COMPLETE

# TRA NSP ARE NY

NG OLVED TRAUMA

Written By

## Shea C. Robinson

Posture of a Pearl Publishing

Publisher's Note
This is a work of nonfiction. It depicts, portrays, and represents real people, places, and events. An effort was made to recreate events, locales, and conversations from the author's memory of them. To maintain anonymity in some instances, names of individuals, places, identifying characteristics and details such as physical properties, occupations, and places of residence have been changed. All rights reserved, including the right of reproduction in whole or part of any form.
All scriptures are taken from the Holy Bible, New Living Translation (NLT), copyright 1996, 2004, 2007, 2013 by Tyndale House Foundation

Library of Congress Control Number: 2020914539
Copyright: @2020 by Posture of a Pearl
Paperback ISBN: 978-1-7354306-0-7
eBook ISBN: 978-1-7354306-1-4

Cover Design: Austin Weatherspoon | AustinGraphix | Austingraphix@gmail.com
Formatted by: Success Dealers International, LLC
Author: Shea C. Robinson

Ordering Information:
Special discounts are available on quantity purchases by corporations, associations, and others. For details, contact the publisher. For orders by U.S. trade bookstores and wholesalers contact the publisher at info@postureofapearl.com.

Printed in the United States of America.

# DEDICATION

**M**y mother, Audrey W. Moore, for her relentless efforts to cover and protect me and support my decisions, while providing encouragement.

My father, Alexander "Bey" McCants. I thank him for his pure heart and for showing me strength through vulnerability.

My grandparents Samuel L. and Addie L. McCants and Edmond and MaeBelle Shepherd for passing on their unyielding strength.

To my brother, the late Rayvon L. Grayson Sr. for inspiring me to write by sharing his skillful talent with us, and for the sibling competition to pursue our college degrees.

My father-in-love, Pop Badger for advising me at Gracelawns planning table, to purchase a single burial plot for my late husband, stating I was young and that I would find love again. And for welcoming my husband Eric as his own family.

# ACKNOWLEDGMENTS

First, I give Honor to God for the opportunity to be stretched in my love walk.

I want to thank my Husband, Eric Robinson Jr. for being an excellent source of support for me and teaching me how to pivot towards my daughter in our worst battles, which caused her to let her guard down to love and let go of the pain. I thank him for being a great example as a man, husband, father, and a support to the entire family.

To my parents James and Audrey W. Moore for the being my saving grace. My mother is always there to keep it 100 with me. And no matter the challenge and how it may have gone against her principles with raising children, she never turned her back on my daughter, even after the abusive experiences she endured and witnessed. Thank you for your unconditional love. I don't believe I would have survived without your prayers and overwhelming support.

I applaud my daughter Kiana Moore for her sweet spirit. Regardless of the anger she felt towards her sister for being abusive and disrespectful towards me, she never returned the anger and rage that her sister was giving to everyone in the home. Even when her sister became physically aggressive with her, she never tried to harm her. And for that demonstration of power, I tell her thanks. And now to our unborn granddaughter, Niara Grace, you are already amazing and I'm sure will carry the same spirit of her mother.

To my son James Faucett IV, for being a gentle human being that would give all he had to help someone in need. It was his pure heart that played a major role in him not developing the same hate that he was receiving from his sister that attempted to do major harm to his body. His unconditional love is what keeps him, and his sister connected today.

To my niece Bianca Grayson I love you to pieces. Thank you for always taking the time to encourage your little cousin, especially when you were the only person, she would listen to. I am grateful for your love and support.

To my older sons Charles and Eric, I thank you for me loving me as your own. To my daughter-in-loves Mary Wright and SanTasha Wright, your love and support is greatly appreciated. And to my grandchildren, Donnie, London, Chad, Skylar, and Charlee, you all inspire me.

To my late husband, James L. Faucett III, I give so much credit for teaching me how to fight with grace during the storms of life. He did not let living with Sickle Cell Disease prevent him from living his life to the fullest and sharing that model with us. I am grateful for his presence and the impact he made in many lives.

To my brothers Raymond L. Grayson Jr. Rayvon L. Grayson Sr. (deceased) and Ronald L. Grayson Sr. for being my first friends. Growing up together with each of you was the best experience in the world. I love the way you always covered and kept me protected. I am proud to be your sister. Thanks for playing a role in supporting me during that tough season.

My sister-in-love, Johjuana Grayson, for providing a sense of respite for the family by allowing your home to be a revolving door for my daughter to stay with you during our heightened moments. You always showed unconditional love. Your support was unmatched.

To my in-loves, Mr. Scott, Mom Melodie Hayward and Rani Robinson for welcoming Baby Girl into your lives and giving of your love and wisdom to help guide her.

To my Faucett family, Brian, Tamya and Yvette, thank you for the support. The laughter provided helped to lighten some of those dark moments.

To all my sister friends, Renee, Kendra, Rani, Sara, Connie, and Tanya, you all hold a special place in my heart.

To my Pastors Timothy and Monique Johns and my entire Heaven's Gate family for the countless prayers, support and never-ending love given to our family. I appreciate you for always encouraging me to do more. I am forever grateful for showing me how to declare some things to move mountains.

To one of the greatest therapists, D. Paramore, who could break the layers of our toughness, and guided us towards healing, letting go and moving forward.

To my coach, Tiphane` Purnell, thank you for your patience and guidance throughout this process. Your experience, wisdom and knowledge made this process seamless. You have inspired me to continue sharing my stories.

Thank you to my Beta Readers for their huge commitment to reading my work and providing me with raw and honest feedback.

To my daughter who I will call "Baby Girl", I am grateful for the privilege of having you in my life. Of course, this book is nothing without you. Thank you for the courage of allowing a piece of your story to be told through my experience.

Special acknowledgements to all those that supported my pre-order release on August 22, 2020, for helping me reach 72 sales in my first 24 hours: Audrey W. Moore, Mary E. Jones, Johjuana Grayson, Marina Daniels-Burgess, Kim Geier, Tracy Grayson, Tamara Walls, Danita Hall-Goins, Nicolle Surratte, Tiphane` Purnell, Helen Anderson, Shakyra Drains, Edith Wright, Blondine Redden, Judy Hutt, Troy Younge, Marcie Smith, Cheri Morris, Shirleah Fowles, Glenice Jernigan-Wescott, Renee Washington, Santasha Wright, Lisa Flynn, Ladoris Wiggs, Raymond L. Grayson Jr., Katrina Hindsman, Connie Berry, Raegan Alderman, Yolanda Brown, Nisey Wright, NyKisha Gaines, Sharon Harding, Heather Brison, Robyn Noonan, Linda Martin, Neil Webster, Zita Davis, Rebecca Wierzbicki, Lillian Nix, Irene Smith, Lolita Ashely, Warner Wheeler, Kimberly Wright, Shelly Stewart, Karen Williams, Justen Wright, Sharon Conaway, Dorothea Williams, Warren Brinkley, Linda Carrillo, Melodie Haywood, Nina Anderson, Tanya Williamson, Robin Brinkley White, Natural, Valeria Harrigan, Wendy Alleyne.

# TABLE OF CONTENTS

# INTRODUCTION

My husband died, and I was left here to raise a child that I Loved, but THAT I DID NOT LIKE! Matthew 20:28 just as the Son of Man did not come to be served, but to serve, and to give his life as a ransom for many." However, it was this scripture that reminded me of Christ's love and it became my motivation to not turn away from my child due to her behavior that was causing the family physical, mental, emotional and psychological pain which felt like a doomed disruption in our lives. Part of my mission was to exhaust all I had to be a good example to my children, expose them to great opportunities, and do whatever was needed in attempt to guide them through life.

Because I experienced multiple levels of trauma within a short period and attempted to walk through it demonstrating Gods love and grace and always with a smile, I can definitely provide some guidance in how to walk through and overcome some struggles in life. From being caregiver to my late spouse living with Sickle Cell Disease, raising my younger daughter diagnosed with severe mental illness and suffering domestic violence from a child, to whom I was not the birth mother, to experiencing the tragic loss of my failed attempts to save my husband's life, leaving him dead on our kitchen floor, to remarrying a former love, and loving those that harshly judged my decision to still live after my first husband's death, to later being diagnosed with an aggressive form of breast cancer, with a near death 7-day hospital stay, to being discharged the same day that our house went into flames. I hope to show you through these experiences, how to maintain a strong posture regardless of the storm that you must endure. I could not allow "giving up" to be an option.

What motivates you to not give up?

# CHAPTER 1
# THE BEGINNING

I had just gotten married on June 16 of 2001. I must say that it was a fun, refreshing, and genuine love. My soon to be husband had courted me for over a year prior to his proposal. Initially, we were good friends, and I did not see him beyond a friend. I really did not have a type, but if I did, Jimmy was not it. I always teased him about that later when we would crack jokes on one another. But we always laughed about how determined he was. For example, I used to take my car to a detail shop in Wilmington, which I later discovered that it was owned by his family. It was easy to locate my vehicle on the road because of my vanity tag, which was Shea-1. He told me that his brother would call him whenever Shea-1 showed up at the shop. He would come and detail my car by himself and put a little extra work into it. I did not know this until we started dating. Another thing I didn't know was, he used to hang out with my oldest brother, and he would always tell him, "Man, I'm going to get your sister." Although I did not remember him being at my oldest brother's wedding on 9/11/94, he was still interested after seeing me in my bridesmaid dress with my big belly, due to give birth in December. It did not matter to him. He saw what he wanted and was going for it.

Fast forward to late December of 1997: our paths crossed at a party titled the "Players ball" This was hilarious to me as we had on matching colors as if we planned it. I remember wearing a black sweater with red leather pants and my black, knee-high boots. He was wearing a red sweater with black pants and red boots. This coordination thing would later become a trend and our signature mark. However, nothing came from this, which I remembered as our first contact. I remembered him staring at me and asking me a question, which broke the ice. He was cool. We clicked; we danced a little and talked a lot more throughout the night. I was really drawn to his personality and his sense of humor was unmatched, but he just was not the type I would date. He was just a little too slim for me, which was ironic because I was a *slimy* too. Well, by the end of the night, we exchanged numbers, and went on to develop a wonderful friendship. I just kept telling myself Jimmy was not my type.

So, I moved forward in a relationship with my current boyfriend at that time, who had unfortunately backed out of going to my family reunion in Alabama during the summer of 1998. I was afraid of flying so I had planned to drive, but I could not do it alone with my daughter and my niece. Well, guess who I reached out to? My good ole faithful friend, Jimmy. I asked him to come with my daughter and niece to help me drive. This was a turning point I didn't realize then. When we arrived, the automatic assumption was that he was my man, so it was pointless to keep denying the fact that we were not a couple. He was just loving the attention he received with that southern hospitality. I still was not interested in moving forward beyond our friendship. We were just too cool as friends. But you know the saying, that the best of friends; make the best of lovers.

He was such a great friend that remained at a distance, for a short time. However, you could always find us hanging out at different places. Whenever there was a party, we seemed to run into each other. He became my road partner and my best friend who I would share very intimate information. If I needed to take a long drive, he would join me because he loved driving and knew the roads like the back of his hand. It was too funny, because we could be in a different state and he would know all the back roads. I guess that memory came from driving limos for WDAS FM, or as a side job for different limo companies.

We hung out together so much, of course people would assume we were a couple, but there was nothing there; we were just good friends. He never crossed that line with me. Now, I knew he liked me and that there was an attraction, but I was not interested in jumping back into another relationship. But the more we hung out, the more I was just drawn to him. I was drawn to his personality, his smile, his crazy sense of humor, the way he cut up when he was cracking jokes on people would have me in stitches. His ability to interact with various groups of people and cultures was mind blowing to me. He was fearless. It didn't matter who you were, he would walk up to a dignitary, a Pastor, or anyone for that matter, and express his opinion based on the current conversation. I admired that about him.

So, the running comments from my friends became, "Girl, you know that's your man, Stop playing!" And because we were both slim, the other main joke was, "You two sticks are going to create a fire if y'all get together, it's gonna be like two bones just clacking back and forth." I would just laugh, and be like, "Y'all stupid". But, as we continued to hang out, we grew closer, and things became more serious. Everything changed in my mind after hanging in Philly, with a couple of his friends, at the club where there was a different vibe of party on each floor. It went from the reggae, to house music, to straight hip: Here is where we had a great time dancing for hours. Now, in route to the clam bar is when our game changing kiss took place while riding in the back of the SUV, which was so memorable that if I reflect now, it stands out to me even today. I can remember at the time how thick, soft, and moist his lips were and how I literally felt like I was melting in his arms at that moment. I had to pull myself together quickly, because I got scared that he made me feel that from a kiss. Afterwards, just the two of us closed out the night or morning with breakfast at the Denny's back home. We talked for many more hours about anything. It came to a point where he was just like enough is enough. He asked in sort of a sweet but inpatient tone, What are we doing here?, You know I feel, I've shown you how I would care for you, so how do you feel about trying this thing out?" I simply replied with something like, "Yes, I want to try and see how things go." This is where we both made a commitment to step into a relationship.

Jimmy did not waist anytime with his decision-making in our relationship or with anything else. He created this beautiful atmosphere at his parent's home, inviting all my immediate family and close friends, where he unselfishly proposed to me on his birthday, September 21, 2000. I said, "Who does that?" Well, James did that! I thought to myself that he is an all-around good dude. Now, although my flesh did not want to say, "yes" to his proposal, I had already heard from God that he would be my husband. Now, this was not a smooth walk, as some of my friends expressed their concerns about me moving forward with this marriage, because of his diagnosis and he was not working. I completely understood every concern expressed, especially being raised, for most of my life, by a single mother, who exemplified strength and independence. Marrying a non-working man did not seem logical. But the fact of the matter is, I was being led by what I didn't realize was the Holy Spirit. I just knew this was a God ordained union. He proceeded to lead the way with making the wedding plans. I mean, he watched The Wedding channel, HGTV, The Food Network, or any channel that involved wedding planning. He got a marriage book and really did his research. I repeat, there was no wasted time. As you can see, we got married within nine months. I realized that part of him having aggressive timelines was the fact that he lived with Sickle Cell Anemia (SS type), and he did not think he would be on this earth very long. For those who may not know, "Sickle Cell Disease (SCD) is an inherited blood disorder, where the red blood cells become hard and sticky and look like a C-shaped farm tool called a "sickle". The sickle cells die early, which causes a constant shortage of red blood cells. As these cells travel through small blood vessels, they scrape the lining of the veins, get stuck and clog the blood flow." This is called a Sickle Cell Crisis, which destroys the internal organs with each occurrence and is very crippling and debilitating to anyone living with SCD. This can cause other serious problems such as an infection, acute chest syndrome, stroke, and even death. Now, I'm sure some people were thinking, why would I marry this man that carries a disease with such a potentially deadly prognosis? All I could say is my actions were purely spirit led, and he had won my heart. So, I was more than willing to accept the responsibilities and the unexpected challenges that would come along with this illness. I mean, I thought I had some previous experience, since I grew up around my aunt, my mom's baby sister, who lived until age 29 with the same illness.

Because of this illness, there were talks very early about having children, but I was not open to it then. We had my seven-year-old daughter for now, so I thought we were good. Even if I changed my mind, I still wanted to wait a couple of years before having a child, since we were just getting adjusted to this newly married life. So, we continued enjoying this honeymoon phase. But guess what? That phase ended abruptly. Just 5 months after our marriage, on November 22, 2001, I experienced the sudden death of my father. This was one of the most difficult things I have ever dealt with in my life. My Dad was the most intelligent, loving, kind, generous, funny, and giving person you would ever meet, that made a major impact in the community with the youth and those in cosmetology. About a week later, our lives came to a temporary halt with my husband telling me that family court called him in, or he received a letter to come in for DNA testing to determine the paternity of a child. I was just thinking to myself, "what the heck is going on!" We were not even 6 months into this thing. I don't remember if he told me any background information about the woman, because it was just a blur as I was still dealing with the blow of death. I was like, "really, my husband is being tested along with several other men to determine if he is the father." I had to chuckle with much disappointment, because I could hear the voice of the talk show host, Maury, saying, "He is the Father." Just the thought of this happening now was crushing my heart even more, while dealing with my father's death. Then, my detective skills kicked in because I started calculating the timeframe. We started dating towards the end of 1999 and this child was believed to been born in September 2000. The wheels were turning in my head and we had some intense discussion around the topic at hand. However, if the child was his, there was enough distance to believe his encounter with this woman ended before we officially became a couple. But if I could be honest, I prayed the results were negative. I just wasn't ready yet. I knew that it sounded so selfish, but that's just where I was. We were still adjusting to each other from the perspective of living under the same roof now and with blending our families together. He did his very best to ensure I was okay, so I did not place any unnecessary pressure on him because he was already feeling the pressure. The day had come, and it was time to get an answer.

# CHAPTER 2
# THE GOOD OLE DAYS

Well, the results were 99.9% positive. I thought to myself; "this fool would be the father". I felt as though I needed to get over myself, shift my thoughts, be a supportive wife, and now a new mother. It was only the right and Godly thing to do. When I tell you, this process was so swift it had our heads spinning. There was no time for us to really prepare in advance for this drastic change that was about to take place with bringing another child into the home. However, I realized this was not new to me because I had seen my mother make quick adjustments to care for other children a few times. And that comforted me, knowing I would be just fine.

So, let me set the tone a little regarding the background of Baby Girl. December 2001 we were introduced into each other's lives. And by April 2002, my husband had full custody of his daughter. Within those four months, we went back and forth with visiting her at her godmother's home where she was living. Remember, she was just two years old when we got her. We found out she had been living with her godmother off and on and then permanently, since she was 18 months old. God mom was a young, sweet, single parent, raising her own child and unselfishly taking care of our Baby Girl. We found out that she, at some point, was good friends with the biological mom, which is how Baby Girl ended up at her home. We later started bringing Baby Girl home with us on the weekends so she could become familiar with us and that we all could acclimate to the changes to come. Her presence added another level of happiness to us. The apprehension that I felt was shrinking, and I recognized, once again I was recognizing God's process.

Now, my husband mentioned nothing, but it was my initial thought she would come to live with us at some point. So, I asked him "why are we going to visit your child, why not get custody and raise her". I had no clue I would later have feelings and thoughts of regret. The court process on this case was the fastest I had ever seen. Once he filed his paperwork, they contacted all parties, which of course included God mom and Baby Girl's biological mother. They had to appear in court to possibly sign over her daughter to the newly discovered father of her child. Although it was very painful for the God mom to let go, she agreed with her dad having custody. Of course, the relationship would continue, we were just changing authority and doing what we thought was best for Baby Girl.

The day for court arrived. He was a little nervous because the courts usually favored women, because we were not sure what her biological mom's response would be. No one had seen or heard from her this whole time. So, my husband and I arrived and while walking into the court building together, we split up once we found out he had to go to the 3rd floor. He needed to be on time, so he took the elevator, which I don't do, so I took the escalator. Now, just about two steps in front of me was this young brown skin woman, bopping and shaking, and saying out loud as she looked towards me, "I can't wait to sign this girl over to be with her Dad, that's just what she needs. And I won't have to worry about nothing." Now I had never met bio mom or even seen a picture, but at that very moment, I discovered that this was Baby Girl's mother. I couldn't even respond or say anything to her. My heart was a little hurt she appeared so excited to let her child go. It wasn't what she said that shocked me, it was her dancing and moving her body as if she was at the club. She was more than willing to sign her child over to my husband. I tried my best not to pass judgment, because I did not know her back story. And at least she was willing to allow my husband to take custody of Baby Girl.

I could not enter the courtroom because I was not a family member. When they all exited the courtroom, I could feel the heaviness of God mom for having to release her, Biological mom was overjoyed, and Dad was excited as a kid in the candy store, smiling from ear to ear. Although it was in our favor, this whole scene was traumatizing. This just hurt my heart because I could clearly feel her biological mom was broken, and this innocent child would be a victim of her abandonment. So, Baby Girl wasn't living with mom, and now she is being stripped from the only safe place she knew with God mom and she was immediately handed over to my husband at the courthouse, with no resources of treatment for what she might need because of this transition. My husband was so excited. But as a mother, I was saddened for the godmother who had been raising her and a little pissed by her mom being so willing to let her go, but I realized later it was all part of God's plan. Anyway, prior to the court date we had gone clothes shopping for Baby Girl, as we were already believing that the Judge would favor my husband. He was so tickled that we took our daughter into a courthouse bathroom, put on her new outfit, and we went on our way. She was officially and permanently added to the family. The added responsibility would not matter to me because it was normal in my household to always see my mother helping to raise other children.

It was humbling to get to care for this adorable two-year-old girl, with beautiful thick curls, a huge smile, and dark, sparkling eyes, with her beautiful long lashes. She did not speak many words. As a youngster, I would play with the babies in our household and teach them to speak certain words, which they could get after repetition. It was always enjoyable to see a child learn and watch their eyes twinkling as we praised them for doing good. And to witness this 2-year-old not saying many words was a little puzzling. We were already talking and teaching her, while we played. Instead of allowing her to point to what she wanted, we taught her to speak and identify what it was, that she wanted. And just like that, her speech became clearer. She was talking constantly, and from that point she never stopped, which was an awesome progression, and hilarious to watch. We discovered from God-mom, that a doctor or therapist advised, that Baby Girl had behaviors of a child that had been abandoned in a crib, left to fend for herself. Hearing this was a little concerning and it would expose these behaviors as she got older, which came from the trauma that she endured.

I immediately claimed her as my daughter. We did not believe in using the word Step as we referred to our children, but we left it up to Baby Girl to flow with her comfort level in what she would call me. It would be her decision to call me Mrs. Shea, Mom Shea, but she decided to start calling me mom. It was the sweetest thing and seemed so natural to her. However, I believe since she heard her sister calling me all the time, she adjusted to her environment. Now, it was important she felt like this was home. I could not imagine how traumatic this must have been to her. She was too young to verbalize those emotions. We also had a conversation with our oldest daughter to explain how she was getting a new sister and that we are becoming one family. Her heart was so pure that I knew she would embrace the change. Her eyes lit up in excitement. I think she felt like she was getting a real-life baby doll.

Although, I thoroughly enjoyed when I was pregnant with my daughter, I was thrilled to know that I did not have to give birth yet. We now have this new little person without the birthing or waiting process. It was a joyous occasion for me and us all, being able to nurture and love her. Going shopping with my oldest daughter to purchase toddler clothes for her new sister was fun and allowed me to bond and share with her the adjustments we have made for her sister to come home. Having Baby Girl in our lives reintroduced us to preschool, toddler parties since our oldest was eight years old. And now we were drawn to a new group of families with toddlers her age. Both of our parents and siblings immediately welcomed her as their own grandchild and niece. But I must say that his mom was over the moon since her son had a biological daughter.

Now prior to any dramatic change in Baby Girl's actions, we created many wonderful memories with her, with trips to the beach, various vacation spots, functions with the church, family, and friends. We loved dancing, singing, and playing games as a family. Especially the pool parties at mom-mom's house when she was little. It was so cute watching my girls play together. My oldest daughter was into dance, cheerleading, and stepping. So, we had a ball with Baby Girl, trying to teach her some moves from the step squad and cheerleading team. Baby Girl was always off beat because she never got the rhythm thing down, but we had fun trying. Even though, other family teased her, she felt comfortable dancing with me and her older sister because we did not make her feel that she did not fit in the group.

She always tried to mimic her older sister. My oldest daughter did not have any rhythm as a tiny tot, so I registered her with one of our local dance studios and boy was that helpful. It helped to build her confidence in herself and to perform in front of a large audience. Well, my younger daughter wanted the same, so we attempted this a few years later, at about 5-years-old. We placed her in a ballet class and then a hip-hop class. Now, we knew she was on the rhythmless nation side, but we had help to build up her confidence in that are so no one could tell her she was not good enough. However, she was removed from the class, because they stated that it was too difficult for them to help her remained focused and she was a constant disruption to the other children. These were the same behaviors that I was noticing at home, but I did not want to press to hard so soon.

Baby Girl was so empathetic and observant. I loved this about her. She took time to study the things you liked and would remember everything. So when it came down to birthday ideas for anyone in the family, she would talk so fast and say to me, "Mom, we can get mom-mom this, but get in this color, and her favorite food is this." She had skills in that area, even at a young age. I found her to be very creative and crafty as well. She was a great party planner. As I noticed some real changed behavior. I realized it was always there, but I tried to utilize things she was good at to try to keep her focused. Her presence brought us a sense of happiness, but we didn't realize it would be for a short period of time. With the joyous anticipation I felt after we brought her home for the first time, a negative shift took place at home, which eventually blocked some of my memory from retaining more of the good ole days. And today I can see how this form of trauma would impact my responses to certain scenarios and some of my inexcusable actions. Let me reiterate how excited I was about having her in my life and in our lives. Her laugh and wide grin could make your heart smile. So, who could believe this little human being's behavior would expose the darkness that was rooted in her from the unknown trauma that had not yet been diagnosed?

During my reflections, I have discovered many missed opportunities, which makes me very emotional now, because we could have created different results if we had known better at the time. For example, based on the neglect that we knew she had experienced as an infant, we could have sought out a therapist then, and been more proactive versus reactive which is detailed in later chapters. This has been a learning process. And through sharing parts of my story, I hope that It could help to prevent some unnecessary challenges that someone in a similar situation might experience.

I want my readers to know what I learned and to do the following:

1. Keep a diary of your family interactions to help retain and pass on memories. It is not too late to begin now.
2. Document your current family health and mental history, and share with family, which can be beneficial in tracing the source of unresolved trauma or possible hereditary illnesses.
3. I learned that I could do better job of being my sister's keeper. Regardless of our personal beliefs we should demonstrate genuine love, compassion, and support.

Shea C. Robinson

# CHAPTER 3
# **THE TRANSITION**

Transition is the process or a period of changing from one state or condition to another.

When I think about the stages in the process of a pearl forming, it is not attractive at all. However, the result leaves the mind to wander how such an ugly beginning can produce such beauty in the end. The pearl's transition is one we could all stand to model as we go through trials in our lives. Well, in this period of my life it felt as though we were not going to have a beautiful end. My transition felt like it was going from bad, to worst to a nightmare. Much like this quarantine we are under due to this tragic pandemic we are living through, the anguish just never stopped. It was that unbelievable and the unmanageable pain was emotionally distressing from my point of view. There was a phrase I learned from a teacher, "Good, better, best, never let it rest, until your good is better and your better is best." Basically, she was saying to put your best effort into any and everything you do. So, with that in the back of my mind, I had to deal with the hard truth that I did not always see my daughter as good, nor did I respond good, as we shifted into this unexpected crazy zone. So, those short-lived good ole days became a memory that I can no longer unfold. This transition happened quickly, and what we would begin to witness left our heads spinning. But I would have to exhaust all my energy to do whatever was necessary to help improve our situation.

First, there were some things that happened early on that I noticed, but I chalked it up to her being a two-year-old and being in or living in a new environment. For example, it was hard to get her to eat with a utensil. She always tried to eat all types of food with her fingers and rather quickly, as if someone were going to steal her food. We had to reassure her by telling her, "It's ok, take your time, as there is plenty of food if you want some more." And then, there was the hoarding of food in the bedroom and anywhere she could hide something. Thank goodness, I found all the old food before it invited some unexpected guests to the party. After locating the food in her jewelry box and other cute hideouts, it did end the fruit fly invasion. These were just some little things that were indications of the possible neglect that she experienced. Again, another missed opportunity to seek some assistance before matters got worse.

However, the manipulation and lies began when Baby Girl started eating all the snacks after Dad had already explained to the girls that they could eat the snacks, but not all in one day. Yes, Yes, Yes! It started with snacks. This became a huge issue, because my husband assumed that my older daughter was taking them because she was tall and thought that only she could reach them. We had heated discussions about this issue because I would not allow any accusations, especially if we were uncertain. It wasn't fair. My daughter said to me and with passion "No, I didn't take them." after I asked about the snacks. I knew she was telling me the truth and not because she was my daughter, but I could sense it. I also knew that Baby Girl was the culprit. But for him, it was logical that the oldest was taking all the snacks because of her height, since I tucked away the snacks in the highest cabinet. I could not say what my gut knew because I did not want to come across as being biased. See, I worked during the day and my husband was home when the girls got home from elementary and pre-school. I found out he wasn't allowing my oldest to have any snacks. This didn't sit well with me. I didn't want this to create any division and become a, "my daughter, his daughter" situation, I needed to be strategic, so that my husband could see the truth without me making an accusation. This was very sensitive, especially as we were working to blend the family.

I switched my oldest daughter's bus stop from our home to my mother's development since we lived very close and advised she would help do little chores until I picked her up after work. I also noticed my oldest doing more than what we needed to help care for her little sister. I just wanted to be very careful and make sure we did not place too much responsibility on her with being such a young girl. In addition, I was trying to protect her from holding any resentment towards her little sister once the truth came out about those snacks. Please understand, either of us couldn't care less about them eating the snacks, but for my husband, it was the principle of the matter, we did not tolerate lying. So, not long after the oldest was going to my mom's house after school, the snacks still came up missing. Whenever he asked Baby Girl about them, she immediately accused her sister, but the kicker was she had such convincing stories for anyone to believe. She had you questioning yourself at times. But it became evident, that Baby Girl was lying. Dad started counting the snacks when it was just the two of them in the house and that's when he finally caught her in lie. There was never a trace of snack trash. The moment he addressed her while we were together, Baby Girl gave me the evil look that could kill. But she never admitted to anything. That look, I would never forget. He later apologized to our oldest for not believing her and automatically assuming she was taking the snacks. We still had to figure out where she was hiding the trash. While checking her dresser drawers, we heard something crunching as he picked up her socks, which were rolled in a ball. Baby Girl hid the candy wrappers in the sleeve of one sock and then rolled the set in a ball. This was deep, that at just 5 years-old she was that crafty and smart enough to cover up the lie, and very well. This might have been funny if this had not created such an issue in the household. It took the cake when Baby Girl continued to deny this and blame her sister for putting the wrappers in her sock. This was unbelievable to me. I was not used to being around a child that was this crafty. I grew up as the youngest with three older brothers at home and we did some stuff, but this here, was very deceitful for a youngster.

There were other strange behavioral changes that started with me and appeared to occur when we were alone, so I did not have any proof of what she was doing. For example, I discovered the word "No" got a different response from her. She threw temper tantrums when she was alone with me. It was unreal to witness that kind of behavior because I must repeat to you all, I was not used to it, it just wasn't normal. I just remember sitting in the living room couch saying, "what the hell is this mess here!" I was like, I am being punked! This has got to be a joke. All I did was tell her no to something I do not even remember, and Baby Girl lost her mind. She was screaming at the top of her lungs, "I hate you! I want it! and NOOOOOOOOO." while forcefully throwing herself back and forth across the floor and kicking and punching the floor as well. See, let me tell you all something in the house I grew up in and all the other houses in my family, we did not show off or act of character. If we even coughed or looked at our parents or another adult wrong after being told No, we already knew it was trouble for us. We didn't know what a tantrum was, and if we did at that time and acted on in, please know, that all hell would break loose on our butts. So, when she threw the tantrum, I was shocked but mainly confused. I did not want to respond with beating her, which is what was instilled in my brain and what me and my husband both understood growing up. All I could do was pick up the phone and call her dad and by the time she heard his voice, she instantly stopped. I had some choice words under my breath. This is when I knew it was going to be drama, because she gave this weird look and this smirk on her face as if she was laughing and pointing the finger at me, like, "haha", I am about to make you look like a fool. In the back of my mind I was thinking, this is wild. It did not know how I was going to move forward.

These actions and behaviors only intensified day by day it was the same behaviors with the tantrums, the lying, the manipulation, the hoarding. It just went on and on and became very overwhelming. Every time I told my husband about what she was doing and the things I was noticing, she would not display that in front of him. So, I'm sure it was hard for him to believe because she was such a sweet girl. I felt like she was trying to make me look like I was crazy. This took a toll on our marriage early on. It was not until one day my husband tricked her. She always played us against each other, for example she would ask me for ice cream or some kind of snack and if she had a good day, I would tell her, yes. However, didn't realize my husband already told her no. And for a long time, we were not checking with one another as it related to her getting what she wanted, especially if her actions did not deserve it. On this day, I believe she asked for one of us to take her outside and play or something. Now mind you, Baby Girl had just gotten into trouble at preschool, so my husband already said she will be punished and could not go outside. Well, the second he closed the door to run an errand, and I literally mean the second the door clicked, she asked me if she can go outside. I told her to repeat to me what your dad just told you? She replied with "No." She said, "I am asking you." in a very nasty, sassy way. The mouth on this little person was too slick to believe that she was only on five years old. However, I told her again, "THE ANSWER IS NO!" and when I tell you it was like watching the exorcist, as she transitioned into a whole other person. My husband did not make it to the car before he could hear her screaming and hollering. He walked back in the house. She never heard him come into the room. But, when she finally looked up and saw him, those crocodile tears stopped in an instance. My husband did not play those games. He believed in that old school discipline, but that would not help. This became a lot deeper than either of us had experienced.

Let me go back just a little as a relates to the beginning of her early diagnoses. Once my husband got custody of our daughter, they gave him paperwork about her current condition. We were pretty much advised because of the neglect of her biological mother, that our daughter now had a developmental delay. They compared her to a child who had been consistently left alone in a crib to fend for herself, no food, just a bottle. They advised us she may have attachment issues, since she never bonded with her mother. At about three years old, we had her in a preschool. I will never forget Miss Wilson. She was the most patient instructor/teacher that I have ever met. She showed our daughter so much love when other programs did not want to take a chance. But even with the most patient group of teachers, Baby Girl's behavior eventually led to her being kicked out of that pre-school program as well. They gave us written documentation of how she had been verbally disrespectful with all the teachers. She terrorized the students by taking their stuff and hitting some children, and whatever else she can do to intimidate them. I mean we got calls 3-5 times a day at least, to address her behavior and many times, they excused her from school. I started worrying if this will get any better because it was not looking bright at all. This continued until she was kicked out of the second and then the third preschool program finally connected us with a behavioral therapist. We needed help and it felt like we were not getting the therapeutic help we were begging for, especially at home. She was very young, she was just three years old, but they felt like an exception needed to be made for all the behaviors she had been displaying.

I believe some hate displayed towards me had to deal with the fact that I was not her biological mother. Although, it appeared she had no memory of her mother based on her responses to prompted questions. My husband and I decided not to share the full story with how he gained custody of her, until we thought she was mature enough to understand. However, a family took it upon themselves to share information with

Baby Girl without our approval or presence. A portion of the information came back to us they told her, "You know, that you have two Mommies". I don't believe he even listened to the full story, because he was so agitated, and was ready to shut that person down immediately, because they had no authority to overstep his decision as her biological parent. So, of course, I'm sure Baby Girl felt like we had either lied to her or were holding back on specific information. This may have been another turning point in some behavior displayed, influenced by what was shared.

My husband managed all her appointments since they needed to speak with a legal guardian in certain scenarios. I was doing my best to attend all of Baby Girl's appointment, but this soon became very taxing as I worked full-time, plus over-time, taking care of home, we worked in ministry together. But I spent more time as a caregiver to my husband, when he would be stricken with a Sickle Cell Crisis, which could land him in the hospital for a minimum of 7 days to about 14 days sometimes.

So, fast forward back to the age of five. We found a psychiatrist to evaluate her. He said she was one of the youngest patients he ever evaluated. He immediately tried to diagnose her with having multiple personality disorder based on her actions in the office with him. Now, I did not want to accept, but I was thinking to myself, wow! he might be right based on the things we witnessed. I sort of chuckled at first, because the doctor was in amazement, but then my parental protective skills kicked in to protect the image he was attempting to place on her. This is where I struggled a lot, because although I agreed with some of the report, I didn't want the system to make her a statistic. Regardless of her behavior, I was always going to advocate for her. So, the doctor's pre-mature diagnoses were formed after meeting with Dad and I first, then with our daughter. It was his strategy to pull us all together after he met with us separately. Once he pulled us all together, he said that it was her reply to his question that was a sign that her behaviors could fall under multiple personality disorder.

I'll never forget the moment that she displayed this strange behavior in front of the church members and it was an interesting moment because she also did it in front of her dad, which she had never done publicly like that. So, it was like the sickness or the illness was progressing at this moment. We were sitting in the front pew and she was misbehaving with me and to my right was our pastor's wife. When my late husband realized it was her making all the noise he walked up to the front of the church with this smooth stroll, and with his belt in hand. He gave a hand motion to my daughter to get up and come to him. Now, I whispered to him, that everything was fine. He ignored me and then looked across at my out First Lady, as she gave the hand motion for him to stop. If you could've seen the look on my pastor's face, I got up and I ask him please don't beat her, he responded and said, 'My Mom beat me and I had Sickle Cell! She ain't going to die". However, he showed her grace based on my request.

So, these were just some small signs where the behavior was shifting before it became extremely intense.

What I want my readers to know:
During my reflection, I wondered if I could have taken a different approach with the challenges we faced. I realized there were some factors that I may not have considered while in the midst of a trial. For example, I had the wonderful benefit of being raised in the same household with my siblings. Unfortunately, Baby Girl was removed from the first home that she knew with her biological mom and her brothers, to later living with her godmother and godbrother and then being removed and placed in our home within the first two years of her life. And then two years later after her final placement with us, she now becomes the middle child due to the birth of my son, which is her father's name sake. I am certain there are adults that would not be able to function properly with that much abrupt movement. I could not imagine what could have been going on in Baby Girls mind in those moments. I needed to fully consider her position each time before I reacted in my emotions. I later learned that the neglect she experienced so young caused some permanent damage to her brain.

Suggestions for those in a similar experience:
1.  If raising a non-biological child with a mental health diagnosis, think about taking a parenting class for some additional guidance.

2. Always consider the child's mindset and position during a crisis moment.
3. Do your best to take time to respond to the situation and not be reactive in the moment.

Shea C. Robinson

# CHAPTER 4
# SPLIT

This chapter shares short stories in non-sequential order of some behaviors that traumatized our household and other individuals. In addition, it will highlight some of the missed opportunities that we make as parents, teachers, and adults to help improve the health of a child experiencing the said challenges.

The school described my child as disrespectful because she would argue with the teachers and was noncompliant. She would frequently steal items from her school that me and her dad had to return. I hated this because it was so embarrassing. Because I'm sure these teachers thought this is the kind of behavior that she is witnessing, but that wasn't the case. So, we had to pick up her face take her back with the stolen items and do the right thing. They also wanted to describe Baby Girl as a bully in the classroom, often very threatening to other children on the school bus. She has been physically aggressive towards classmates, kicking and hitting the children. She has even been suspended from the school bus because of abusive behaviors towards other students. It has been difficult for her to sustain peer relationships and would often shut down with frustration because her friends did not stay around long at all. She would resort to name calling and spreading rumors about that person because they no longer wanted to be her friend.

As a mom, this became very difficult to watch because all she wanted was love, but she did such devious things to push people away, that it would have you thinking she is getting what she deserved. Honestly, it made you think or say things like "that's what she gets". But I had to remind myself that it's not her, but that its' the behavior.

The question that was always asked of me was, how much abuse was I willing to accept? How long was I going to allow this behavior to torment the family? Some of her manipulative behaviors match the girls from the 2009 movie titled, "Orphan". If I could explain the evil that my daughter gave us, this movie sums up just a portion of the devious nature. But even with the hate she gave, I always attempt to return with love. I knew the word said, "do everything in love". I could not understand why I was allowing such things to continue, as I would have not tolerated this from my older daughter and my son that I later birthed in 2004.

When our son was born, this added more fuel to the fire for Baby Girl. She was no longer the youngest and now we had another infant in the home for us to love on. My husband was just beside himself, especially being there to witness his name sake being born. I mean he literally caught him with one hand, while assisting the doctor with her glove, as I pushed him out. My son wasn't waiting for anybody. Please know I was very cautious to never leave my younger daughter alone, because she was already showing signs of jealousy.

As little brother started walking and talking, Dad felt comfortable enough to leave them alone and play, while I was at work. I begged him not to leave them alone. But sometimes he did, when he didn't have much control, especially whenever he had a Sickle Cell Crisis. The pain would leave him motionless in the fetal position because he could not move because of the great pain. This required immediate attention. He needed oxygen and his medication to help relieve some pressure, but it would never take away all the pain, especially in his lower back area. So, it was understandable and with that I had to teach them at a young age how to call 911, if Dad was too ill to respond. This was a very tough decision to make. I called home as frequently as possible to ensure everyone was safe.

One day my husband caught Baby Girl, dragging her brother across the carpet. The rug burns it left were so bad, that part of his skin had come off. This was enough for me to make additional arrangements to take my son to none other than my mother's home during my work hours, to ensure his safety. My husband felt terrible that he had dozed off when that happened. There was no one to blame as it related to him feeling sick, but we had to be very cautious. Sometimes my Mom had to attend her appointments, so she could not be available all the time. In these moments both the younger ones would need to be home with Dad. The abuse continued against her brother. We had this bay window in the kitchen, and I used that space to place my decorative candles and little knick-knacks. Now my daughter knew these candles were gifts to me and were not to be burned. But in a jealous attack, Baby Girl lights my candles and pours the hot wax on my sons back just as quickly as my husband could step away to use the bathroom. My husband said our son's screams captured his attention and he disciplined her after she attempted to blame her 1-year-old brother for the burns on his back. My mind went way left, because I'm thinking about the, "what else could have happened" scenarios, like what if she poured the wax in his eyes, what if she lit his hair on fire. I was thinking to myself, what was my little man thinking at the time and what long term affect could this have on our son. It was time to make a change, as my son's life was at risk. Yes, it was that deep for us. We hid all the lighters and matches to the fireplace, which is what she used to light the candles.

My husband and I came to an agreement that my mom would help watch our son during the day, until he was old enough or ready for daycare/preschool. My mom eventually made a room for our son in their home. Because of the continued behavior throughout my daughter's time with us, my son maintained that room, even now at 16, that is his second home. It was so necessary for them to be separated because we never knew when my husband would experience a sickle cell crisis. This was hard because my husband was feeling like he wasn't equipped to keep watch over his son and that simply was not the case. I did the best I knew how to encourage him out of that way of thinking, since he had no control over when this illness would attack his body. Using my job benefits, they referred us to Dr. Reyes by our behavioral network. We are still in the year of 2005. Her strategy was slightly different from the other doctors at the time, as she had just reviewed our written documentation and then interviewed our daughter first. When she finally pulled us into her office, she explained her process and eventually told us and I quote, "DO NOT leave them two alone, she is going to severely harm her brother." She also informed us that based on the artwork Baby Girl created during the session and further discussion with her, it was clear that Baby Girl hated her brother because he was stealing all the attention. This was a sigh of relief to finally receive clear and direct instructions from a doctor since this was always my concern.

Please understand that for the next three years, we experienced a countless number of other issues as the mental illness progressed. For example, our son has a major food allergy to peanuts and our entire family was aware. We even had a safe plan in effect if something ever happened. So, his allergy was no secret. Although we kept peanut butter in the house and safely stashed away in a zip-lock bag, we only ate when he was out of the house. Well, I don't remember why Baby Girl was upset this time, but as I was cleaning the room this day, I found where she had hidden the peanut butter underneath his bed. Now, I got to a place where I had to clean the room daily because of the hoarding, so I knew the peanut butter was not there earlier. Can I tell you how angry and how hurt I was thinking about what she could have done with the peanut butter in my son's sleep? Understanding that this was and still is life or death for him. I was so hyper, and unable to control my language now, because it was time out for trying to be calm and nice. She was placing his life in jeopardy. I could calm down a little, enough to ask and not assume what she was going to do with peanut butter, and she admitted she wanted to see what would happen. And I lost again, to the point of anger bringing me to tears, and I realized it still does, as I'm writing this today. This was so vivid to me because I remember making the call to my husband while he was in the hospital, recovering from a Sickle Cell Crisis, and saying to him, "She got to go! She had to get the hell out of here." I was in a space that I just could not take this anymore. I just felt like, what's next. So, of course, I trashed all the peanut butter and anything that was peanut related. I wasn't taking any chances, just in case one of us slipped up. We could not afford anymore mishaps.

My oldest daughter, who was very caring, mild-mannered, respectful, and acted as if these issues with her sister's behavior didn't bother her much, even when my husband was ill. But it was obvious by her actions, as she attempted to step in the role as her brother's protector, ensuring that she was always present if we had to step away briefly or if we became distracted by any household responsibilities. She even showed love to her sister, by engaging them both with a game or watching a children's program. Whenever my husband was in the hospital, and it was just me and the children, she was always extra helpful around the house, but I never wanted her to carry the weight of my responsibilities. I needed her to remain in her youth. She had already been involved in various dance programs since the age of 3, like ballet, jazz, and hip hop, which was necessary so that her focus was not always on trying to be a protector. We continued her involvement with the church choir and later she taught the younger children dance. My daughter had taken on my traits, that whenever things appeared out of order, she went straight into work mode to see how she could help her mother. My husband and I were similar, as we did not sit in pity whenever he was ill, or when Baby Girl had caused some destruction. We knew how to have fun aside from all the pain we would endured, we needed to stay sane through prayer, and keep our children balanced with us playing games, taking pictures, dancing as a family and making videos.

At times, I was afraid to sleep, in fear of what she might get into if I did. I made sure that she was asleep before I laid down for the night. So, for a little peace of mind and so we could all rest peacefully, we purchased an alarm to put on the outside of her bedroom door. If she left the room after we have all gone to bed, then we wanted to hear right away. There was no more room for error, as we had to protect the safety of everyone in the home. Talk about overwhelming and exhausting, because I still did not sleep well due to being scared, I would not hear the alarm if Baby Girl woke up. It was not normal to live like this. I was still walking in faith and power through prayer, and it still felt like my peace was being stripped. I had to be an example and fight through the feelings of anger, bitterness, disappointment, and that give up spirit to show my family this illness, whether medical or mental, would not destroy us. We had to walk in victory when all we were seeing and experiencing at home, was destruction.

What I realized is this behavior because of mental illness was going to show up no matter what. Baby Girl later became infatuated with fire. One day after going to work, dad was getting our younger kids ready for school, and my older daughter caught the bus before I left for work. Well, dad had Baby Girl downstairs eating breakfast, while he was getting our son ready upstairs. By the time they were on their way downstairs, my husband caught her running out of the front door with her coat, and then noticed the huge flames coming from the kitchen, where she started the fire in the trash can. Overwhelmed with anger and excitement, he told me that he leaped from the middle set of steps to the bottom and grabbed Baby Girl by the hood of her coat and pulled her back into the house before he attempted to put out the fire. But he could snatch the fire extinguisher off the wall and put out the fire before it spread to the walls and the ceiling. Most of the damage was contained to the trash can, so there was no need to make a call to the fire company. This incident just showed how we could NEVER relax our guard, because we had hidden the matches and lighters years before.

These recent behaviors changed the dynamic of how we moved forward getting the proper team to guide us through these unexpected and life-threatening events. My husband decided it was time to call the Crisis line where they came to evaluate her after the fire incident and based on the results, they highly recommended we take her to the Rockford Center for residential treatment. This was year 2008, she was only 8 years old. With all these displayed behaviors, so many left untold, I still struggled with the decision of having her placed into a residential facility. After arriving, completing all the paperwork and meeting with the staff, we explained to Baby Girl that she would stay for a few days and the reasons why. All I can remember is seeing the fear in her eyes, and although the look shifted to anger, my heart ached for her. It was hard to leave because I felt like we were failing Baby Girl and that we left her unprotected. I didn't want her prescribed with a bunch of medicine, but I knew something was necessary. I know most people close to our family, thought I would be relieved to just have a break without her in the home for a few days, but it was just the opposite. It felt like this was a sick mother/daughter relationship. I was the one she disrespected often and the aggressor with some physical altercations, but hated to see her get disciplined, even though, I knew it was necessary.

It's amazing that you really don't know how you will respond to these kinds of challenges until it happens to you. We can judge all day about what you won't tolerate because I've done the same thing. Never would I have thought I would still allow anyone in my space after death attempts have been made against my loved ones. We always heard of many stories, whether on the local or national news, or a TV show where a child living with mental illness killed someone or the whole family and it usually started with issues like ours. In some instances, the parents talked about how they let their guard down or just never thought their child would take it to the level of death. Well, that became my mindset, "to always think of the worst that could happen", so I didn't miss the mark.

After talking with my brother-in-law, it reminded about the bathroom fire at her paternal grandparents' home. She walked down the hall to use the bathroom. She came out just a few minutes later, walked back down the hall and sat with her grandparents as they watched TV. Her Pop-Pop started smelling smoke coming from the back room. As he walked down the hallway, he could see the smoke seeping from the cracks around the door. He tried to open the door only to realize that she had locked it. As the smoke thicken, Pop-pop had to kick in the bathroom door. They found she had lit a candle and burned the toilet paper, by the time he got the door open the fire was about to travel to the curtains. Thank goodness they had fire extinguisher in the kitchen as was able to put out the fire quickly. Her mom-mom was so afraid that my husband was going to beat her, that she begged her younger son not to say anything. Uncle was not having that. He picked up that phone quick to tell what she did. He was like, "Yooooo, Jimmmy, you need to beat her m...fkn @ss. Guess what she did?" What I realized early on is that most of the family would always resort to beating, but that would not work with these behaviors. They would only intensify. Now, my brother-in-law was and still is a funny character. He brought much laughter to relieve some pressure due to the pain that we were experiencing, and he is still a great support today.

Now, Baby Girl was so skillful at storytelling that this behavior convinced my mother, who is not very easy to persuade, of the things she had told her. My daughter was upset she was not in a wedding on her god family side and told my mother the grandmother pushed her down for no reason. The passion and commitment that she displayed while telling this story was so interesting that my mom called my husband and said, "Jimmy, you need to listen to her because that woman could abuse her." My mom had the kind of relationship with my husband where she could pick up the phone and share her opinions without him being offended because he loved her as a mother as well. So, he replied in his calm, cool manner and said, "Mrs. Audrey, she's lying." She asked, "Jimmy, how do you know she's lying?" And he responded in his serious but comedic way by saying, "because her mouth is moving." He had gotten to where he believed nothing she said anymore. So, to prove his point, he called the grandmother on a 3-way call with my daughter by his side. We learned from therapy to address these issues head on. He asked the grandmother if she did what our daughter was accusing her of, and our

Shea C. Robinson

daughter spoke up and said she never told my mother that story. There were just way too many stories to share. Some of these stories, could have become detrimental to the individual accused. We knew more help was needed in accurately diagnosing the behaviors and getting the help to guide us all into better approach of managing this illness. So, for the next 3 years, the behavior just became exaggerated, resulting in numerous school suspensions, residential stays, excessive hollering and banging her body parts against the walls, graduated to self-inflicted physical harm. The question was always, "when will it better?" But things continued to get worse. We had to believe for better.

My husband was excited to finally receive a referral for our daughter, in the last quarter of 2011, to be evaluated at a Consultation Clinic within a major children's hospital. This experience was the best, as it related to what she and the family would need long term along with resources to follow-up with afterwards. The goal was to get her the best treatment for her to live a successful life. It was December 2011, when we received the final 15-page report where Baby Girl was diagnosed with the following: 1. ADHD, Combined Type, 2. Conduct Disorder, Childhood Onset, 3. Mood Disorder, Not Otherwise Specified and 4. Rule out Reactive Attachment Disorder. This report confirmed what we were already undergoing. We were given a thorough and descriptive synopsis, which stated the following:

> We have a high degree of concern with Baby Girl's emotional and behavioral functioning. Her presentation includes a few severe issues, including concerns regarding her safety and the safety of those around her. Thus, we recommend that Baby Girl and her family pursue intensive comprehensive intervention that includes psychotherapy and psychiatric intervention. The venue for treatment should be based on Baby Girls functioning, and should minimally include intensive outpatient therapy, with the possibility of day treatment or residential treatment. Baby Girl and her family have attempted to engage in outpatient therapy in the past but have been unable to consistently engage in treatment. With the severity of her presentation, significant interference of her functioning across settings, and the families' previous failure to remain in outpatient therapy, we strongly recommend that she be placed in an intensive outpatient therapy program, such as one at the Terry Center, where both psychiatric and psychological services are available. Baby Girl's

treatment should be coordinated with education efforts. Thus, we encourage her family to share the findings of this report with teacher and school officials once she returns to public school. In school, her I.E.P. should have many built in behavioral and emotional supports.

Our families' inconsistencies that were mentioned in the recommendations, were because of my husband's unfortunate stays in the hospital. And since I was not a legal guardian, we could not continue with those sessions. This is when I strongly considered legal adoption to handle these important matters, whenever my husband was ill because of a Sickle Cell crisis.

I showed a great deal of patience, even in moments when my response was not indicative of my behavior, but trust me, I was meditating on doing what was right. I was reminded of one of my scriptures in James 1:2 "Consider it pure joy, my brothers, whenever you face trials of many kinds." So, no matter how difficult the challenges, I encourage you to do your best to remain hopeful and happy during the process, because things could be worst. Be grateful about where you are not, and smile because you're still standing.

To my Complete Transparency readers, Parents or Caregiver in a similar situation, I encourage the following:

1.  Identify what brings you peace. **Example**: For me at the time it was prayer, worship, listening to uplifting music, shopping, and spending time at the water.
2.  Seek counsel immediately for you and the entire family to help navigate through the challenges and help to guide each family member through their personal emotions.
3.  Join a support group to help with a reduction of stress, anxiety or feeling of isolation as if you're the only family going through some strange times.
4.  Choose wisdom over the heart's decision. Allowing our hearts to take control of our decision making could lead to more trouble, but I believe wisdom protects. Unfortunately, I made the mistake of allowing my heart to stop my husband from making the wise choice of releasing Baby Girl to a treatment facility, which could have prevented some unwarranted trauma.

# CHAPTER 5

# SUDDEN DEATH
# AND MARRIAGE

In the midst of all the chaos, our hearts were crushed, and the loss of my husband devastated us. His death changed the whole dynamics of the home. If the sudden absence of his presence weren't traumatic enough, living with the fact that I couldn't save his life was almost detrimental to my sanity. At times, all I could see was the image of me on the kitchen floor doing chest compressions until EMS arrived. It was the morning of January 14, 2012 at 8:45 am, just 3 days before my son's 8th birthday. My son woke me up that morning and he said, "Mommy wake up, Daddy is downstairs sleeping by a knife." I looked at the clock because that was always the first thing I did whenever I would find my husband sick in the house, as EMS always needed a list of information when they arrived with the ambulance. I had a method, where I gathered all his medicines, grabbed a pre-printed, laminated list of the meds, I dressed my husband, put my dog in the kennel, and close my children's door so we didn't wake them, as I did not want them to always see their Dad in crisis. But I was not the one that found him, so I just ran down the stairs and I paused, looking into the kitchen, where I could see my husband appearing lifeless as he sat on the stool, with his head on the counter, looking towards the bay window and his arms were dangling at his sides, appearing to be heavy with fluid. I was in complete fear, thinking that my worst nightmare is happening before me. I calmly called 911, while calling out his name with no response. Fear crept in me for a bit which is why I shouted to my 16-year-old daughter, "Kiana come here please, I need you to check Mr. Jimmy's pulse." I finally moved off the steps and walked towards my husband with my daughter, as EMS is now talking to me and asking questions like, "Is he breathing?", "Ma'am can you hear me?" I popped back into work mode and responded to the call. I placed them on speaker while my daughter and I picked him from the stool and laid him on the kitchen floor. As we were laying him down, I heard his breath come out of him, and I was like, "Yes, he is breathing", but then in the back of my mind, I realized it was just a gurgle. Now on his back, 911 is telling me to start chest compressions immediately, but I took a quick second to try to open his mouth just in case they told me to do mouth to mouth, I noticed his tongue had already cleaved to the roof of his mouth. But I wasn't giving up. I remember 911 saying, "Count out loud, 1, 2, 3 and stop, 1, 2, 3 and stop" I was pressing and counting quietly, because I was trying not to deal with the possible reality that my husband is gone. "Ma am! Keep counting out loud!" I was counting, and the tears are drenching his white T-Shirt through my hands as I continued to press on his chest. This was, what I called, that last intimate moment with my husband. I wondered if he could hear me, or if he could feel me, as he was transitioning right there before my eyes. This was the scariest moment of my life, yet peace was present in that moment. I could hear my then 7-year-old son dancing in the next room, which I thought he didn't have a clue as to what was going on. What seemed like forever on that kitchen floor, ended quickly when EMS arrived and pushed me out of the way to do their work. I was escorted upstairs by the police, my parents had already arrived, and our street was full of fire trucks, EMS, cops, and an ambulance. I was frantic because I was not allowed back downstairs. I was told that I could not ride in the ambulance with him because the police had to question me, which I later found out that this was the process when someone dies at home. I knew he was gone.

So, after they finished questioning me, my mom drove me and my older daughter to the hospital, while my Pop stayed with my son and younger daughter who was still sleeping. This was a somber ride. I made phone calls to his siblings and his best friend, and I remembering saying to each of them, "You need to get to the hospital for Jimmy now, because this time is different." All I could think about is my husband is possibly dead. Arriving at the hospital, they had what I called the death hallway and when the nurse confirmed who I was, she began walking us towards that hallway, and I stopped and told her, "No, please tell me now if my husband is alive, I do not want to walk down this hallway, I know what this is, I just know, it's the same hallway they walked me down to tell me that my father died back in 2002." Somehow, we all ended up in the family room and a doctor came knocking on the door shortly after, he said, "Mrs. Faucett, the situation looks very grave. I responded with, "Grave, Grave! What does that mean?" He said, "We are doing all we can." I remember repeating that to him, "Please do everything you can." Later, I remember seeing many family members and friends arrive at the hospital. Shortly after, that same doctor came to deliver the bad news that my husband did not survive while I was standing outside the family room. I was just like, "NO, NO, NO!" What was so vivid to me was seeing my daughter to the left of me and a little ways down the hall, collapsing on the floor in anguish, with my Mom attempting to hold her up and then to my right, I could see one of my nephews sitting on the floor and I could hear him calling other family stating that, "Uncle Jim is dead." I could no longer hear that doctor. My faith kicked back in and I ran to the room where he was because I knew they could do more; it wasn't his time to go. I was praying and believing for a miracle. I ran out of the room banging the walls in the hallway and crying out, "God I Trust You! God, I Trust You!" with the support of my friend Connie, holding me up. He had so much more to share. All I know is, I walked out of that hospital no longer a married woman, but as a widow. My marriage, as I knew it, had died too, and my children's father was gone. I still had to go home to tell my younger children. I had gone back to our home first, as the children were at my mom's. My house was full of people by the time I returned from the hospital. I think I was in shock. I was sitting on the steps next to my friend Renee, as it was her birthday that day. She spoke in a soft tone advising me that I still need to go and tell my children, which I was dreading. This just did not seem like my current reality. Someone drove me to my parents' home. Surrounded by family and close friends, I said to them, "Daddy passed away." My son repeated my words in a painful tone, "Daddy…. died!" I can still hear the squeal from my son, that turns my stomach till today. My younger daughter cried briefly and said, "Daddy's gone. This was the only time with my daughter when I did not think of her behavior, until she immediately flipped the script and accused me of killing my husband after I told them he died. My oldest daughter was so angry with her sister after hearing her make the comment, "I guess I won't be getting anymore beatings." This made my daughter feel like Baby Girl did not have a real love for her Dad. I felt like I lost the balance of what held our home together.

I don't know how we made it through that first day. One thing that stood out to me was when we finally made it back home again. I was attempting to clean up my kitchen and some of my family and friends told me to sit down, and I snapped, crying, and shouting and begged them, "PLEASE, just let me work!" See, it's what I did well, I always kept it moving, so much that my oldest daughter picked up my traits, and just worked, while my First Lady, Lady Mo, helped to manage the crowd that was already forming at my home. Somehow, we decided it was best to leave my two younger children at my parents', so I could sit with my family and friends that were showing up to support and for the funeral that was already contacted, which was a dear friend to my husband. As my poodle stayed close to me, I sat and watched and listened to what came across as noise from everyone. While I loved the company, I wanted to be by myself, but then I was afraid of facing all the pain alone. So, having grief on top of trauma I felt would be very heavy to manage.

As the crowd dwindled away, I became more apprehensive about going to bed that night and too weak to even shower. I don't recall sleeping, but I now cried and tossed and turned all night with my first lady watching over and she slept in the chair next to my bed. That next morning, I showered and the heaviness of his absence fell strongly on me, that I continued to wail out, "God I Trust You", God I Trust You", and banging on the shower walls hard enough to crack the drywall. My first lady, who was overcome with grief and the pain I was released, stood outside the bathroom door, and supported me through prayer. The pain was so great, that it felt like someone was slicing my heart apart with a serrated knife. We lost more than a husband and father, but we lost a friend, our chef, the mechanic, the plumber, the electrician, you name it, and he was that. To make our loss even greater, we experienced the death of many friendships. I believe when my husband died, some of our friends did not know how to stay around me, so those relationships dissolved. It hurt to the core when my children later asked about specific people they loved, that no longer came around.

I had to make immediate adjustments and push through my pain, as I needed to support each one of my children through their grieving process. It was very difficult, since I took on the pain of their grief along with mine. So, I did not waste any time with finding a place for my children where they could express their grief. It was a great service, centered specifically towards children who have lost a parent. I registered for a grief/share program at a neighboring church, which was very helpful. Sharing my experience and hearing other people's story was heartbreaking, but inspiring and encouraging. It played a significant part in my healing process, and I hoped that organization chosen for my children would do the same for them. However, it was just a temporary program and what we all needed was therapy. But how was that going to happen when baby's girl's behavior never stopped, it always dominated the situation? Unfortunately, the behavioral therapy used all my extra time, therefore, neglecting personal therapy for each of us due to our great loss. How were we going to cope with grief and the never-ending affects from Baby Girl's behavior?

To my readers who have experienced a sudden death in the family, please get therapy even if you feel it won't be beneficial. Trauma has a way of creeping up on you. It could come out in the form of depression, anger, fear, anxiety, having nightmares, sleeplessness, constant flashback, or never-ending sadness around a matter. Below are some resources I used to help support the family. However, I failed to get therapy surrounding the grief, as Baby Girl's therapy sessions for the mental illness consumed our time. The continued grief and the effects of the abuse from his sister led to trauma showing up in my son, with some negative and aggressive behaviors that he displayed towards me, which was never his character. We later introduced our son to Trauma Focused Cognitive Behavioral Therapy to help him through the anger he was experiencing.

1. Grief Share Course
2. Supporting Kidds Inc.
3. Healing Pathways

I would also encourage you to get involved with a volunteer activity, which might help towards your healing journey. For example, our family continued with Sickle Cell Walk that my husband initially launched in July 2009. However, prior to his death, we planned a Sickle Cell Walk on a larger scale to bring awareness about SCD to our local area. The goal was to provide education and advocate for adults regarding their treatment, besides establishing support groups for caregivers and their families. My husband and I collaborated with his Nurse Practitioner to come under her organization to begin the process as she had dedicated her life to Sickle Cell Research. On September 15, 2012, just nine months after his death, we successfully launched the first James Faucett III Sickle Cell 5K Walk/Run and raised over $5,000. We celebrated 9 years of success on September 26, 2020 with a virtual walk due to the pandemic. I can say that this entire experience has been very cathartic.

## 360 Degrees (Full circle)

I have matured to a place where my faith drove my actions and decisions. While I am still healing from the death of my husband, a love from my past returns in my life. It was uncomfortable for me at first, feeling the loss and still loving my husband while falling back in love with a man I dated 15 years prior. Some family and friends judged me harshly because I lived my life, but I still showed love to them during the process. I knew it would be hard for others to accept how I went from being married to James, Widowed, and Engaged to Eric within 11 months. However, I was determined not to allow others to dictate my future. I remarried in 2013, just 19 months after the death of my first husband. There is no perfect person, but Eric did all the right things by meeting with my parents and family. My husband was so intentional in how he interacted with my girls and engaged my son. He took the time to take each of them out on various dates to get to know them individually. It was simply amazing how my children responded to Eric, as there was no resistance from with forming their relationships. My son, who did not receive correction well from any other man, was able to receive correction from Eric at the time.

This was a huge responsibility for my husband to step into a ready-made family, still in the healing process of a major death, but he handled it with such a gentle and loving hand.

I knew as I started dating a love from my past, I had a feeling this might be a little much for my children. Heck! It was a lot for me to understand what was going on. I mean, I had just lost my husband and feeling the effect from my daughter's accusation of not saving his life when I was doing chest compressions on him on our kitchen floor. But I could feel God was healing me from the trauma of the sudden loss of my first husband and bringing forth this Man from my past to pursue this relationship, which I knew was a divine connection. It was difficult because while I was still in love with my deceased husband, God was allowing me to love my soon-to-be-husband. I was scared, I was nervous, and I was concerned about every member of my family, from my mom who looked at my late husband as a son, from my in-laws, close friends. What were they going to think? I wanted to try to protect everyone's feelings. But, my children, they were my main priority, and I was concerned about what they would think. Thoughts like, will they think I am forgetting about their dad, do I Not care about their feelings, are they ready for me to move forward? But in finding myself, I became free, knowing it was okay to continue living and have their hearts in mind. Again, God was doing something in my life that I did not understand. After Jimmy's death, my daughter's behavior had intensified immensely and now God returns a former love back into my life.

Eric, also a member of the church, asked about being a mentor for my son. Now, I'm certain that somebody may think that his request had motive, but knowing his character, I knew he was genuinely concerned for the state of my son's mind and he was strategically placed at the same church for this reason. It was an answered prayer when he asked me about mentoring my son. Eric simply explained to me that while he sat during my late husband's funeral, (which I didn't even know he attended) he heard all the good stuff about him, and how much he loved me and his children, and what a good father he was, and what his son meant to him. He felt compelled after praying that God use him to guide my son as he goes into this next phase of his life without his Dad. There were folks I could've asked to mentor my son, but I went to God first. So, I prayed He would send somebody to help my son, to be there for him, to guide and encourage him and teach him about being a man. In addition, my son would need a demonstration of what it looked like to respect and protect the women in his life, like his mother, sisters, grandmother, etc. So, when I got the phone call and request to mentor my son, I simply cried and gave God the praise. Eric did not know, but he was responding to my private prayer request. See, I was especially scared for my son because he was with his Dad every day. I was hurting for each of my children individually, but especially my son. I knew that no one could ever replace his dad, but I also knew it would be crucial to his growth to have a strong man in his life to mentor him outside of our family, not knowing that he would be my next husband.

So, long after his interaction with mentoring my son, our conversation shifted in the direction of rebuilding a tight friendship into a relationship. It felt weird at first, but soon the transition became comfortable and a little easier, especially after receiving two prophecies about a man of God who was coming into my life, or should I say, coming back into my life. The first prophecy was from a family member who said to me, outside of my husband's funeral, and I quote, "Your next husband was at this service." I looked at her like she was crazy, but I was numb with no further thought about what she said until three months later.

The second prophecy occurred after I was asked to speak at my friend's nephew's funeral. I was emotionally terrified because her nephews service was scheduled to be at the same church where we had performed my late husband's service. This fear was shared with my Pastor's and they gave me very specific instructions to follow so I could still support my friend and press through the fear. I was told to wear my clergy collar and sit at the front of the church, so that I could leave right after my assignment of reading the Old and New Testaments. My Pastor said, "do not sit in the pulpit!" I arrived for the service and did exactly as instructed, however, when the officiant saw me in my attire, he asked if I was on the program and invited me to sit in the pulpit. I complied because I did not want to seem rude. As the service started, I quickly finished my assignment and returned to my chair in the pulpit, waiting for the opportunity to sneak out. Well, that opportunity never came and after staying for the entire service, the officiant asked all clergy on the program to come back up to share words of encouragement to the family. Can you imagine the shock? But, I had to pull my emotions together and get up and inspire the family in the midst of my visible grief.

Finally, the service was over. I hugged my friend at the end, told her that I could not attend the burial and that I would be returning to work. She was ok with it because she was not going to the burial anyway. Somehow, I ended up in the funeral procession to the burial, because I thought I saw her car, as if she changed her mind. After the committal, the officiant, asked all clergy to place their flowers on the casket and I left the gravesite immediately, while all the family and the rest of the clergy was still there. It became clear that I was being led back to the church for a reason, as I drove back to the church to apologize to my friend for not being able to stay for the entire program. She responded with, "you already told me that, what are you doing here?" I told her that I did not know. Finally, I was leaving the church building again, and as soon as I turned around, the officiant, who I thought was still at the gravesite had stopped me. He began to prophesy to me, stating that, "God was going to bless me with a man that has the heart of a pastor, who would tame the lion inside of me, and not to worry because it was going to happen fast." His words were a little overwhelming to receive, but it was confirming at the same time. Therefore, this eased my comfortability to move forward into what would happen later.

But personally, I wasn't released yet to go public with our relationship until I heard a word from my first lady at my church. She was sharing a story about how she prayed often about an affliction that impacted her daily living, but it wasn't until she received, and I quote, "The full love of God," that was she fully healed. That was an "aha moment" for me. This allowed me to accept God's full love for my life. I became okay with getting married, being a widow, and getting engaged within 11 months. I finally understood this process was not about me. So, the concerns for my children became a non-issue. Initially, my main issue was with my youngest daughter not being as accepting and possibly vindictive towards everyone, with me moving forward in a relationship, especially since she constantly accused me of killing her father. The trauma from our relationship was at the forefront of every move I would think of making.

The moment I started to share this portion of my story, it surprised me that it inspired other women who had been divorced for some time and wanted to marry again; it gave them hope. This was just more confirmation that we can't keep our testimony to ourselves.

I give my husband the utmost credit for honoring the legacy of my late husband and accepting the position of genuinely loving and leading this family. I don't know of anyone who would willingly step into the challenges that he had witnessed with my daughter. If it were the other way around, I don't think I would do it. I would have walked away before I got involved. I thank my husband for moving in the power of love and not fear.

# CHAPTER 6
# SPLIT PART 2

My husband set out to get the best services for Baby Girl's treatment prior to his unexpected death, which he accomplished. However, it left me there to handle what became a daunting task. The feeling of being alone, abandoned, and unable to pray, I only knew how to cry out to God. While carrying my children's grief, I needed to feel a release from the fear of parenting alone, being a widow at 38, raising a child diagnosed with mental illness, while ensuring our safety and attempting to hold on to my job to sustain the support for my family. It was crucial that I did not isolate myself, so that I did not sink into depression. My goodness, the pressure was overwhelming, but I didn't have any choice but to push through because my children needed me to be whole while in their brokenness. Staying connected with my family, and the church was my saving grace. Since I struggled with reading the Word for myself during this time, it was vital for me to remained in an environment that fed my spirit and encouraged my soul to keep living. I remembered being so desperate with trying to prevent myself from going into a dark place, I literally stood on my Bible with my bare feet, telling God I will still stand on every Word in this Book to keep and sustain us. And I surrounded myself with like-minded folks.

Even in my husband's death, mental illness was trying to steal the little bit of peace we were hanging onto with the memories of his presence. The behaviors attempted to overtake us during these weak moments. The heat was turned up because now, dad was gone, and she knew my discipline was not the same. Every morning presented a level of difficulty, as there was always some drama Baby Girl created. The illness caused her to be very hyperactive, impulsive, and always in attack mode against her brother, sister, or myself. At times, she would tear up stuff to agitate me. I would holler at her, which led to her screaming, hollering, banging her head against the wall or kicking and trying to break anything, so, I would have to grab and hold her to prevent her from going completely wild. My oldest daughter would try to keep her brother calm while he was also yelling at his sister to stop acting like that. My oldest daughter would be heated, but I didn't want her to interject and get involved. As I always tried to control the situation. I didn't want anyone else to step in and accidentally hurt her in that state or hurt themselves. It was my decision to keep her, so I took the brunt of everything. After she calmed down, I usually had to shower again and change my clothes because they would get sweaty from tussling with her. Based on her behavior, I had to determine if her actions required a crisis call before I took her to school. Either way, it was necessary to go into the school to meet with an onsite therapist or counselor to provide an update on her morning. These actions became a regular part of the morning for us because it was almost every day, which was draining. It's amazing to me I didn't wise up sooner and hold off getting dressed until she went through her morning drama. She usually acted up when it was just about time to leave the house. I knew those actions were intentional.

Sometimes her actions came across as pure evil in my eyes. Speaking of intentional, most of her behaviors were designed to harm the other person. For example, a portion of this story is still very clear to me. I know it was a school night, as my son was taking a bath with the door open in preparation of the next morning. My oldest was multitasking in her room watching TV and doing homework. We had a peaceful couple of hours. I guess it was a little too peaceful for Baby Girl, because the next thing I remember, was her walking past the bathroom and shouting to her brother, 'That's why your dad died!" in a very nasty and hateful tone. She said it as if he wasn't her Dad. Well, of course this struck my son's heart and he tried to jump out of the tub to retaliate, yelling, "I hate you", but I was already in motion and leaped towards him and held him as he cried uncontrollably from the pain. But as I was trying to console him, my oldest daughter got upset, and asked, "Why would you say that to him, what is wrong with you?" And then Baby Girl went off in a rage towards my daughter's room turning over her trash can and other stuff. My oldest said something to her sister like, "Girl, you're about to get hurt." So, I ran out the bathroom soaking wet from the tub, leaving my son and told my daughter to calm him down for me and I dealt with the little one's behavior as she attempted to tear up her sister's room. She had already thrown the trash around, which is when I grabbed her and told her to, "Clean up this mess now", but I'm certain I was not nice about it. Because here I go again, tussling with this teenager to prevent her from doing more damage to the house or harm to herself or us. I told her she was not leaving that room until she cleaned up all the trash. She refused and tried to walk away. To avoid putting my hands on her, I stopped her with my body weight. Of course, she attempted to push back but wasn't strong enough. This was crazy, because this continued until she got tired of fighting and eventually cleaned up the mess she made. Afterwards, I made her apologize, then sent her to bed.

It got to a point where our household needed a break, my mom's household needed a break, and the only other place I could send her for respite for the family. My daughter could no longer visit because of the aggressive behavior she displayed towards one of the newborn infants. Because of her jealousy and anger regarding the attention the baby was receiving, she pushed the stroller down a small hill, causing the stroller to flip over with the baby screaming. Therefore, her trips to her God family ended temporarily.

Writing this book required me to dig deep into my memory bank. There is so much to remember, so I reached out to some of my family. I talked to my mother who reminded me of an instance, when I asked her to come put the kids on the bus so I could get to work on time. While waiting at the bus stop, my son was in line to be the first to get on the bus, but Baby Girl also wanted to be the first one on the bus. So, as the bus came around the corner my mom said she pushed him in to the street in front of the bus. My mom grabbed her by the hoodie to try to stop her. Somehow, my mom grabbed her hand and while she had her hand, my daughter started twisting my mother's thumb in the opposite direction. Because of this, my mother's previous arthritis condition flared up, which caused her thumb to swell three times the normal size. It has been eight years since that happened. Every time I look at my mom's hand, it makes me sick, because I feel guilty about the stuff that I put them through because I tried to continue to raise his child again. All I wanted to do was see her win in life. When my mother called me to tell me about the situation, I turned around immediately, as I was just five minutes from the home. My mom did not allow her to get on the bus and took her back to our home until I arrived. I snapped when I got there, I was just so pissed of how she disrespected my mother and tried to harm her brother. Thank God for FMLA, which was my friend. Although I needed to be at work, I had to take time to have this behavior addressed and contact the crisis instead of her current therapist, who was not very helpful in those moments.

I didn't have time for me. I spent most of time attending therapy sessions, going to the school to meet the educational diagnostician, and on-site counselor. I spent more time responding to incidents where she was either the offender 98% or the victim 2% of the time. And unfortunately, that small percentage where she was the victim was documented by the school as her inciting the incident. However, the other person got violent because they could not manage their anger based on the things my daughter was saying to them, causing her to be the victim in those few scenarios.

They were many times I would go back-and-forth with defending all the wrong my daughter had done in school. I was always being called into the school about something that happened, whether she put her hands on someone or started trouble. At times, the school was so frustrated that their response would start out negative. But even though I knew she did it, I still advocated and did my best to not allow the school to label her a bad child. I was so regular at the school, all the staff and most of the student were familiar with me. Funny, the staff often thanked me for being a great support, but I was doing what I was supposed to do.

One day Baby Girl came to me claiming that another female student had been bullying her. This student had pushed her out of a line, spit in her face, and the teacher did nothing about it when she told the teacher.

Baby Girl knew how to stir me up. Initially I was furious, but then I had to take a step back and think that this is probably another lie. But she swore up and down that this girl did this to her. I literally asked to almost beg her several times, "please don't tell me this, if it is not the truth. I don't want to go to the school to find out that it was you." She was adamant as she's always said, "I'm telling the truth for real this time, I mean it." I refuse to go into school again only to look like a fool. This was the pattern I kind of knew what I was getting into when I would go to the school to defend her, because I felt like it was my job to support her no matter what. This is where I think the trauma affected me because I already knew the outcome of her story was going to be a lie, I went so hard for her, I think I believed the lie, when I knew it was not true. It always came down to whether it was a teacher, the principal, the nurse, the on-site cop, or the therapist. It didn't matter, because it always came down to the investigation showing Baby Girl as the mastermind, the liar. To put the icing on the cake when everyone was brought into the room to tell their story, she would always flip the script on me and admit it was her the whole time. Can you imagine the frustration and the anger? Then I just felt crazy as hell, like why am I continuing to do this to myself? I knew the answer, I knew what the response was going to be, I knew she was the one who started the fight, I knew she was the one who created the issue, I knew she was the instigator, but still I fought for her as if I knew she was innocent. I poured a lot of energy, a lot of my time into this.

See, I didn't like hearing those teachers talk about how bad my daughter was. I would let them know regardless of what the issue was, I am her parent, and I will support her wholeheartedly.

She was in middle school; I got a call about her being a victim of bullying by this young man. Now, she said he had pushed her against the locker and kicked her. When someone came down the hallway she was on the floor as if she were in severe pain. She refused to move until the on-site school resource officer came to pick her up and place her in a wheelchair. She was taken to the nurses off because she was hurting so badly. Therefore, I had come to the school to pick her up early and take her to the doctor to get checked out. The report was, there was nothing visibly wrong. Normally, there's nothing internally wrong, however, I thought it was important to follow up based on the report I received, but I knew in the back of my mind I was going to get the full report later. Let me go back a little. I had just told her that I'm going to stop running to her aid because it always turns out that she was the culprit. Well, she must have shared this with the nurse and the SRO, because when I arrived at the school, he was concerned I would not get her checked out. I said to myself, this mess is ridiculous. Well, I also told her previously I would always support her, so I continued to advocate and press charges in this situation based on her story. About a week later during their investigation, the school finally looked at the camera because the boy who was being accused denied everything. He said he was not even near her at the time of this incident. They found that my daughter was harassing another student in the hallway at that time. I received a call regarding this new information, and I suggested we have a meeting to include her therapist, so she could address my daughter's issues once they showed us the tape. When we came together to have a full team, parent-teacher meeting. We all viewed the video privately. When they showed the video my daughter, I was not surprised she denied it and said, in a quick but jolly manner, "That's not me!" Some of those teachers were baffled to the point where they questioned themselves. All I could say was to myself was, "Wow!" I interjected to ask, "Why are you questioning the video, when you know it's her?" I was confused by their actions. The therapist explained the behavior she was displaying. It came down to this young man almost being charged with a crime. It was the video that saved him from being convicted, and it revealed another vicious lie from my daughter. It was situations like this where I told her she's going be the little girl that cried Wolf one day. I said, "When you need me to believe you, I won't, and that's going to be a sad day for you."

Her actions continued, and really put us in danger. We were leaving the Food Lion supermarket one day, along with my son. I noticed a group of little girls walking towards the supermarket, and I didn't realize they were coming in our direction. Next, I realized my daughter was already in the truck. There were several young girls and two boys that stopped me and said, "Ma'am we know that you're her mother and we just wanted to say to you that your daughter's mouth is really reckless." I had to pause for a moment because it shocked me that this group of young ladies were bold enough to approach me, a grown woman, about my own child. Normally, I would not entertain a child question an adult, but I could tell they needed to be heard. So, I listened to them because they were respectful and passionate. I remember it was the smallest young girl who did all the talking. I remember her saying something like, "No disrespect, I just want to let you know your daughter has been saying a lot of things about a lot of people and all of us think she might get hurt one day." I told her I appreciated her honesty as it takes a lot of heart to do this. Of course, I took that opportunity to try to show peace and share a little wisdom with them. I simply shared they might want to be a little careful in approaching adults about their children because the results may not be as pleasant as this encounter. I expressed how uncomfortable I was just continuing to engage in the conversation. But I suggested, if they had any further issues with my child, to do their best not to resort to violence and report her behavior to a teacher or principal to prevent them from getting into trouble too. This young lady was adamant, she said, "Ma'am! I don't think you really understand. Her words are vicious, and she is really reckless." At that moment, I knew exactly what she was feeling, but I would not express that to these children. That was my queue to end this little chat, by still encouraging them to not let allow someone's words to lead them to violence, don't stress over the small stuff, and I advised them to enjoy the rest of this beautiful day. Now, here I am giving these kids advice and I'm having the same challenges. They went on about their business and just as we were pulling off my daughter put down the window and shouts something smart. Her brother responded, "See, that's why they want to beat you up." I stopped the truck and checked her immediately.

I remember she overheard a family member discussing a concern about a church member. When we got to the church the next Sunday, she took it upon herself to speak to this grown individual and ask them if they were okay, based on what she overheard in a private conversation. First, I was always taught as a child we did not get into adult conversations. But she took it to the next level and discussed what she heard during an adult conversation. This was an intentional action on her part because she knew how we felt about doing stuff like that. In addition, she knew it was a sensitive topic, which could've caused this individual to leave the church. The results of this could've gone all the way left but thankfully everyone were adults about the issue. And the individual knew our discussion was rooted in love. Now, I know you're probably thinking, what was wrong with us having this type of conversation around her anyway? I didn't think we had to be mindful of everything we said around her, but we did. It was like being in Prison in our own home. I had to find private areas or send her to a different room or send her outside so I could take care of business that I didn't want her to repeat even down to the very minor things. I became more irritated and frustrated with the situation of raising my child.

One of my family members judged me harshly based on my parenting style with her. We developed some strict rules for certain scenarios based on previous history with her behavior. But it wasn't until he had his own experience with her, that he realized why we have implemented some rules. He had the opportunity of witnessing her attack on me after taking her hair out. Every couple of months, I would get her braided during the summer. This made our process for leaving the house for our many appointments much easier. So, it was that time to take out her hair. While helping to take out her hair, my rings got caught in the pulling out and it jerked her neck on accident. She snatched away in such an aggressive manner that she pulled my arm, so my natural reaction was to pull back with strength and my hand was released. Then one of the craziest things happened, she was already on the floor, because I was sitting on the bed. Her body turned towards me and I could see she was upset; she did the wildest thing and jumped at me, biting me on my inner right thigh. I'll be honest, I smacked the mess out of her so she would let go. So much occurred the one during this tussle. She turned around with such hate and rage her eyes. And from the position of where she was on the floor, she kept kicking me. To stop her, I took my foot to step on her leg, but in doing so I later realized that she had kicked off half of my toenail. I didn't discover this until I notice the blood on the wood floor.

By this time, things were already out of hand. My goal was to keep her from doing more harm and trying to keep calm, so I didn't lose it and intensify matters. My brother was in the house, heard the noise and came running. By the time he arrived, I was trying to remove her from the bedroom. She was biting my left arm through my shirt. I was so agitated I could not feel it. He attempted to grab her, and she told him, "get the f&$K off me". I told him I got it. I didn't want anyone else to get involved, potentially react in rage, and get themselves in trouble. He called my mother, who showed up quickly. My mother begged me to call the cops, but I was scared for them to show up while she was like this, as I was afraid the cops would hurt or even kill her. No matter how she treated me, I always had her best interest in mind.

This behavior was always quick on the draw to come up with anything to bring all the attention to them. For example, my mother was at our house with us as I waited for my daughter to get home from the school. I had an appointment, so my daughter was going to leave with my mom. Prior to my daughter arriving, my first lady/pastor's wife showed, and we were laughing at the top of the steps. Now, I could see her getting off the bus with the appearance that all was well. She was smiling and I didn't see any negative energy. She came into the house, saw us having a little fun and immediately told me that an eighth grader came to the front of the bus and smacked her in the face, and started crying. See, she knew how to trigger a response from me. I asked if she told the bus driver, and she'd said she did nothing. My mother picked up on it right away and suggested that I not overreact. I jumped in the car and caught up with the bus just around the corner and stopped the bus. I got on the bus and politely told the bus driver what my daughter told me. The bus driver said, "ma'am, your daughter was the one that got up from her assigned seat in the front, she was the only child on the bus with an assigned seat, and walked to the back of the bus to antagonize the older students. She jumped in the face of the eighth grader to get disrespectful, so the other student smacked my daughter in her face. This was a pattern where she would play the victim. She would set the scene by only telling a portion of the story that did not show her part in the situation. She knew I would always be there to support her and be her advocate no matter what. By the time I came back to the house she appeared happy, skipping around the yard while watering the grass, as if she just did not stir up any trouble.

I literally had to pause and take a break to wipe my tears and blow my nose, because I was thinking to myself, how do I even cope with this process? How do I get through writing this book without breaking down? I've come to realize even in this section, there was a lot of traumas that I dealt with that was just normal to me. And whenever I would share the scenario with the doctors or the nurse or the therapist or even family, I presented all the information nonchalantly. I would be like, "This is what happened this week, she tried to burn the house down, she ran away from school and home, we had to send out a gold alert because she was missing, now she attempted to stab her brother, she tried to cut me with her nails; she did this to her sister, she was abusive in school," I mean the list would just continue. With all these things, they would have to stop and catch their breath because it was exhausting to hear. I told the story as if it was our everyday norm and I didn't look phased by it. People would still see me operating with a smile which to them was simply amazing. The response I heard from others was, "You are very strong," but there was never any respite for me, at least not from the organizations that were designed to help our situation. Of course, I got breaks from the help from my mother and other family members, which were an intricate part in allowing me and the household to have a short break from the behavior. This was saving grace.

We had been in every mental health facility in the new castle county. With each visit, I felt there was less success, behavior only got worse. My daughter has spent so much time in these units, that she knew exactly how to behave she knew exactly what to do she knew exactly what to say in order to get out of the program quickly and it was a regular pattern. But there was never any real accountability to the home while she was inside the facility. So, I have folders and phone folders from the different facilities where the exit plan was only more medicine. At the beginning of my breast cancer diagnosis, the family had enough. No one ever said it, but I do believe they felt his diagnosis came about due to the stress. Everyone came together for this meeting to try to get the help that was needed because I didn't want to let her go. The choices were to rescind my guardianship or find some better help within the system. The organization we were dealing with did not want my child going into the system, so they came up with a plan to send her to a day treatment facility, called Silver Lake treatment. Now I'm thinking to myself, why hadn't we heard of this program before and what a coincidence now that I have considered turning her over to the state that they come up with this great opportunity? She ended up being in this program for nine months. We were told she was the longest day treatment patient they ever had.

She continued to struggle to manage her mood and behavior at home, at school, and in all social environments. She continued to have difficulty managing impulsivity, and her mood was unstable about 75% of the time. Unfortunately, she always struggled with problem-solving and her emotional reactivity was concerning, because it always led to verbal or physical conflict with everyone in the home and especially outside of the home. This treatment center was the first Center that addressed all her issues without first wanting to change her medicine. In addition, there was an accountability record set home for us to document as well, to monitor her behavior at home. When she was at the other treatment centers, she knew exactly what to do to get out, but with this treatment center she had to continue to do the right thing at both the center and at home in order to be discharged. So, when they sent home this accountability record for us to fill out every night for her to take back the next day, you can imagine the problem they created for her. She expressed her hate towards me even more because she felt like I was trying to control every moment or her life, like I was blocking her freedom. However, this was the first sign where I thought there was hope things would improve for us.

I know this might seem harsh that all I could do was highlight all the bad in these moments. And honestly, I could share for days the many stories that we encountered with mental illness. We did not know how to deal with trauma. Unfortunately, there were just so many more bad stories that over-shadowed some of what was good. I thought sharing love was the answer that could help eliminate some of these hateful behaviors. Whenever, my other children wanted to return the same energy to their sister, I always encouraged them to walk in love. Yes, I had my moments when I could not even walk in what I said my actions were rooted in, which was love.

I learned the following:
1. The importance of getting educated on trauma or whatever issue you are dealing with. We needed this at time to understand how to handle certain scenarios, which could have eliminated some unnecessary stress.
2. We should have identified more of Baby Girl's good actions, caught her in the moments and recognized those behaviors since we always recognized the bad ones.
3. Remember that parents, guardians, or caregivers must do self-care which is essential for good health whenever you're in the midst of a tense environment. Initially, I did a poor job of taking time for my own self-care.

Shea C. Robinson

# CHAPTER 7
# **COPELESS**

When I reflect on the moments when I felt that there was no possibility of our situation ever improving, I had to maintain a hope for better through the Word of God. This scripture encouraged me in Isaiah 41:10, that says: "So do not fear, for I am with you; do not be dismayed, for I am your God. I will strengthen you and help you; I will uphold you with my righteous right hand." This motivated me to press, especially since I continued with raising Baby Girl. I knew that all would be well. So, I was not hopeless in the matter, but we were left Copeless for a period because of the lack of successful tools provided to support our daughter and the family during this season.

As I sit and ponder over all the IEP meetings, the therapeutic meetings from the various facilities I remember all the support that was provided, the very detailed instructions and steps on how to help my daughter. I mean we talked about her stress, her slow triggers, her fast triggers, and tips to counteract those behaviors. I'm doing my best to maintain, and I think at the time I never even thought about it regarding getting myself help. But, as I sit and reflect, I needed that time, I needed help with my triggers. I needed help with how to respond and apply these tools to myself.

We went through several organizations for treatment and Intensive Outpatient Therapy, but without great success. Now, every time we received a new therapist, I provided feedback regarding her progress and the things we would do to help aid her progression. Any time she was taken into the community by each new therapist, they asked to advise them of any concerns. Well, in this one example, I suggested to the therapist that my daughter should sit in the back seat, as she does things that are very distracting when we are driving, to where it almost caused us to get into an accident. Well, I didn't understand the purpose of asking, if they were going to do their own thing away. I was questioned and judged for my actions, until they experienced what I was talking about. For example, this one therapist had my daughter sit in the front seat of her 2-door car. How about my daughter snatched the steering wheel and jumped out of the car on this one therapist? I think the therapist was more traumatized than anyone else because she called me to help coax my daughter back into the car. If the assigned help could not provide what we needed, then what were we supposed to do? It got to a point where she overpowered a couple of her therapists. This is where I had to request a change, which ultimately led to a new therapist under a different program. One male therapist that worked with us who we felt was good for her didn't work out because she was attracted to him and was overly sexual in his presence. After further discussion, another change was necessary. So, we lost confidence in the organizations' ability to help our daughter and the family.

Below are examples of a few recommendations provided by therapists whenever we had a crisis. Living in this process was so traumatizing for the family, that my husband, who was educated in addiction, got educated in Social Work, which became very helpful for us later. I am also taking courses to understand the psychology of the brain

| Recommendation | Did the recommendation work? | Responses to the recommendation | What worked? |
|---|---|---|---|
| Do not engage in verbal confrontation or negotiation but respond briefly to her actions. | No, as I was unable to follow. | I was long-winded because of what I learned from my mother. Confrontation was hard to avoid after she had become | What worked was daily prayer, listening to gospel music, engaging with my family like eating, |

|  |  | verbally aggressive and physically confrontational. | dancing, and singing. This prepared me for the day and kept my mind sane to be able to manage all the hell that I knew I was going to encounter just in one day. |
|---|---|---|---|
| Try the time-out method with the freedom of being creative. | No, when Baby Girl had too much unstructured time, the behavior became more impulsive. | I knew that it would not work for our crisis scenarios. We became more frustrated with therapy process. | Provided more structure. Limited her downtime. Gave her the guided authority to help decide consequences and rewards. |
| Withhold desired activities contingent upon doing the right thing. | It did not work because she would just detach herself from the activities and continue with worsened behavior. | I was beginning to accept, with all the recommendations provided, that it was never going to change. | We figured out how to withhold stuff with her involvement of giving a timeline when she could engage in the activities |

| | | | or have her items returned, even if she did not fully do the right thing. (We came to the realization that at times she was incapable of doing the right thing.) |
|---|---|---|---|
| | | | |

My daughter required an increased level of care because of the chronic ongoing mental health issues, so I had to apply for **FMLA** which is the family medical leave act. This system protected my job and allowed me the opportunity to take intermittent time off for the unexpected crises that would occur. There were multiple appointments, many crisis sessions, and visits to a treatment facility, or visit to the psychiatrist, so receiving that time off was important. Just thinking about it is very overwhelming and emotional because I realized I never had no room to exhale. Work, work, work, was all I knew. And to take in all of what we were being dealt with. I just had to go into work mode. I had to get work done, take care of the business, take care of my family and I had to keep moving, never really taking time for myself. This makes it so difficult for me to even press in, and attempt to write this chapter, because I don't want to stir up emotions, I never faced head on.

It seemed like every time she had to stay at the facility, it was only a temporary fix. They made her accountable for her actions while she was at the facility, but there was no accountability from the organization. She just came home with several prescriptions to treat each diagnosis. But where was our help? It just felt like we weren't doing enough to cope with his never-ending crisis. We were living in crisis daily.

Because I never really sat in the toxicity and pain that was created by these mental health challenges, I now peel away the scabs as I dive into these regurgitated memories, causing my tears to flow. Even though I was in these therapy sessions with her, I never took time to get the necessary therapy for myself. I told myself I did not have the time, but the truth is I just never prioritized myself like I prioritized everything and everyone else. Honestly, I believe it was a trick of the enemy to have me believe I was okay. So, I never dealt with my trauma directly, but it sure dealt with me through my moments of physical aggression, which ended up with me punching holes in the wall, or the few blackouts I experienced like becoming angry at very small situations. I questioned why am I still in this? Why did I want her to win against this mental illness battle more than she wanted it for herself? I think I wanted to prove that one psychologist wrong when she told me that, "You would never be enough for her", as she will always be this way. I disagreed with her and believed my faith would win. I see now it was more selfish for me, not to consider what the professional was telling me. I had to come to grips with understanding it is not and never was healthy for us to stay in this situation. We were not healthy for one another and this was hard to grasps, because that meant I would have to let go, and if I let go, that meant I failed her. Failure wasn't an option for me. I was raised to not give up or quit. Whatever I worked on whoever I work with, I applied and gave the best I had to give.

I didn't really do a lot of cussing, but there were some moments where I lost it. When I think of the moments, she put her hands on me or another adult, it just messed with my head, because I didn't grow up like that. There was no way we thought it was acceptable to place our hands on our parents, let alone talk back, or even look at them crazy if we were told to do something we did not want to do. Any time we got out of order, we were put back in order, instantly. See, we knew when we were in trouble, the minute somebody saw you doing something wrong and you heard them say "Oooooo! you gonna get it!" You knew your life might be over. We understood the repercussions of our actions, but with my daughter, that never registered in her mind. When she was wrong, she thought she was right. That was a challenge for me. I was baffled by her thought process. During discussions with my husband and other family members, we had an understanding that Baby Girl did not have empathy for anyone, otherwise she would not continue with the same behaviors towards the people she claimed to love.

Now, when her dad was alive, she knew was going to get a beating if she was out of order. But she knew with me, that I was going to always try to talk it out. She took advantage of that with me, but she never did that with her dad, because she knew she would be in major trouble. So, with that being said, I felt she knew what she was doing, and all her actions were not related to mental illness, but just her being manipulative. I was messed up and confused at the time with trying to decipher what was mental or a behavioral issue.

She never had much success in therapy because most of her therapist never focused on her strengths. The person in that role was ever changing because of the difficulties they faced in dealing with her dangerous behaviors. This process felt pointless to me. I mean this child lived with such Severe Persistent Mental Illness, meaning the manipulation never stopped, the lying, the stealing, the evil tactics, and the abuse from the sickness never stopped. It was unfortunate that we could never decompress around Baby Girl because the behavior always kept us on high alert.

Let's pause right there, I need for you all to imagine living with this every day. I was always living on the edge, wondering what she was going to do or try to do and destroy my life today. How was she going to delay my process with getting ready for work, church, a meeting, an event, a quick run to the grocery store? If I looked happy, I felt like her goal was to stop it. I was just so disgusted and overwhelmed that I thought crazy. Basically, if she was going to be mean and nasty, then it was time for payback. It got to the point where I did not want her around me. We used to take her with us wherever we would go because we knew we could not leave her with other people, without putting them in harm's way. We later realized it wasn't punishment for her but for us because she had the benefit of having us all to herself. I noticed how much happier she was. Well, with the grief and turmoil she caused in my life, I would not continue her having all the fun in her mind. So, when my mother offered to keep her for us anytime, we went out, she hated it. But guess what? It felt good to me. I did not care anymore. I was sick and tired of being miserable and living in misery whenever she was around. It felt good to me that she did not get her way. At the time another family member was living with my Mom, so I knew my daughter would not get slick, because she had more respect for this family member than any of us that played a part in her direct care. There were many times where I wanted her to feel just a little of what she was handing out. So, if we had plans to go out for dinner, she was definitely ordering from the kids' menu, which was usually limited to chicken fingers, fries, hotdogs and mac and cheese, but she had prime rib taste. I was always on the go, so of course, we were always grabbing food from a fast-food restaurant. If she had gotten into trouble at school and I knew we were going to be gone all day, I packed her a lunch from home. She would not benefit from the joys of eating at some of her favorite spots, while she was wreaking havoc in all our lives. At first, I used to feel bad about doing that, but it later didn't matter how she felt. Yes, I know that sounds mean, but I just did not know how to cope in this situation any longer.

In her younger years, her dad would send her back to stay with family in another town for the entire summer, while we enjoyed vacations without her destruction. It's sort of sad when I look back on some vacation pictures and notice she is missing. Those summer trips soon ended after she pushed that family member's infant child over in the stroller because she was jealous of the attention the child was getting. The last group of people she loved, she felt abandoned her. I had so much trouble trying to balance and make some sense of my emotions. I out of character with my responses, but I hated the position I had unwillingly been placed in with caring for her even more after the death of her dad. With all the Hate that I wanted to give, I often allowed love to override it. I repented and apologized to God and Baby Girl for my actions. All the prayer, the love provided, the therapy just seemed like it would never end. I was at my wits end. I felt horrible with how I started treating her because she was just a child. But her mouth was like a 35-year-old grown woman. So, I resorted to letting her see her Own Evil Mirror. You know the saying, if a child bites you, then you bite them back, and they will never do it again. Well, I started taking that approach because nothing else seemed to work. I only purchased the things she absolutely needed. I put the brakes on getting some of her wants. Her punishments were comprised of taking her game boy, Nintendo, and her dolls for long periods of time. Because of the Reactive Attachment Disorder, it was easy for her to detach after not having them for so long. However, I allowed her to keep her Legos, puzzles, and books, because she loved to read and was very skillful at putting together those tiny Legos.

It was difficult to live in a house with these behaviors because I needed to keep track of every move she made. I could never truly rest unless she was asleep or not in the house at all. To ease some stress felt and to allow for more rest, we placed alarms on her bedroom door when she was sleep. I could not go to sleep until she was sleep, because I could not trust her. She would always creep through the house at night getting into stuff. I could not risk her going into the kitchen unsupervised and put something in our food or drinks. She had already attempted to cause a fire in the home. I had to expect anything, so, I did what was necessary to protect the household, so the door alarms added a bit of comfort, which allowed me to get some rest because the alarm was loud enough to wake us up if she walked out of the room in the middle of the night.

Living like this was very unreal for me. I tried my best to always show love, however, her disrespectful mouth made it so hard. Everyone in the house responded to her with the same energy she gave. I knew I had the power to change that, so I always encouraged her siblings to show love and respond in love even when she is being mean. It wasn't fair to them, for me to place this expectation on the other children to show love when all she is giving is hate most of the time. We were all struggling, confused and angry. Somehow, we still had fun.

I knew it was getting to a point where I needed to consider letting her go based on my black out moments. For example, we were driving to get some food from KFC. Right after my daughter disrespected my mother, I was addressing her to let her know her mannerisms we are disrespectful, and I will not tolerate it. I went back and forth with this child so much, that my anxiety overwhelmed me so much I pulled over to have my older daughter to drive. This child continued to antagonize me from the 3rd row of my expedition. My son was in the middle row, and I was in the passenger seat when she said to me, "Forget your mother, I hate you, you f&$@ing b&@$!" All I remember, is both her and I ended up in the middle row in the drive through of KFC. If it wasn't for my oldest daughter jumping out of the car and opening the driver side back door and screamed, "Mom" I looked at her and came out of my rage. After I realized what happened, I apologized to my children for losing it. I was distraught, so I know they were messed up by my behavior. I cried as I apologized to her as well, because now what her behavior was, my response was my responsibility.

Remember the old school three-way call? Well, back in the day, a woman's ministry would call each other on three-way. We would have about twenty-five women in each person call another person and it went on and off. Of course, various topics would come up. I remember for months, I would be on these calls, and finally I broke and shared what was troubling me. At this point, it didn't matter who was on the call, I wasn't concerned about what people thought or said about me. I knew I needed some guidance. I just needed some help. I'll never forget it, I cried like a baby because I struggled terribly with the feelings I was having towards my daughter. I disliked her almost to the point of hating the fact she was in my life causing all this turmoil. I felt sick to my stomach and in my body because I didn't like myself for having those feelings. But I thought I had every right to, I mean her actions turned my life upside down. I prayed and asked God to protect my heart and remove the bitterness and hatred that rooted within me. It was chaos after chaos, and it was time to let her go.

They provided me with a lot of written resources to read but I never really had much time to do any of that because I was always completing paperwork as it related to my daughter, whether it was IEP paperwork, courthouse paperwork, or school documents. So, whenever I had a moment, I just wanted to rest I didn't want to do any research on the behaviors I was already living with.

Historically, physical discipline is what I was used to, but I quickly realized it didn't work. It was important I took time to calm myself I spoke to her and gave a consequence. If we were going to take something from her, we had to have a plan of how she was going to earn it back. When we provided discipline and removed personal items without a timeframe, it made it easier for her to detach from that item. To return was more helpful than just taking it and never giving it back. She worked harder at maintaining good behavior if she knew she had an opportunity to regain her stuff, have the freedom to watch her TV or whatever it was she liked to do, if she had a timeframe of earning that back. But when she did not receive a time frame, it didn't matter to her.

What led to me to wanting to rescind my guardianship was the feeling I could no longer keep her safe. She no longer respected the boundaries of staying within the home. And this reckless behavior could only spill over to her little brother and possibly bring danger to the home.

Because Baby Girl was always making up stories, I knew she was lying when she came to tell me she had been violated, when she was a part of this program, we had her participate in. She went to my mother and expressed some confirming things. Unfortunately, I can't go into great detail here, but can you imagine? I was completely devasted to know she was telling the truth and I did not believe her even with the graphic telling's of the story. All the investment that was made to protect her, we were unable to do so in this situation. I wanted so much to remove the pain she was going through and desperately wanted to do harm to the one who violated her. We followed the procedure and moved forward with an investigation and proceeded to file charges against everyone involved, however, the investigation came to an abrupt end when the one who violated her was tragically killed by the cops in another case. The trauma she still may be experiencing because of this, is unmatched. As for me, it took a toll on me emotionally. I had to seek help from the Lord through my reading, meditation and praise and worship, and I eventually was able to forgive those individuals, so I did not carry the burden on my heart.


Things I want my readers to know:

1. It is vital that you build a team of support, so that you can build up one another during moments of weakness.
2. Never lose hope while in your battle. Believe that you can experience Victory in the **MIDST** of trouble. I did that by doing the following: **M** = Mediated on the Word. **I** = I had to identify who I was in Christ to build my strength. **D** = I

to remain determined to win. **S** = Stand on what you believe. **T** = I Trusted God and the process I had to endure.

3. Remain supportive to your loved ones, even when it's difficult to trust their position.
4. Eliminate selfishness. I learned that I was selfish. Please let's not make it all about us.

# CHAPTER 8
# WHEN LOVE IS NOT ENOUGH

"Your love will never be enough for her" is what the psychologist from the Terry Center told me when Baby Girl was referred for an evaluation after my first husband died. She brought me into the room and made it very clear to me, and stated, "Your love will never be enough for her." But would my love for her through the love of God be enough? I thought it would overpower this sickness. I wish understood mental illness better at that time because I could have approached my next steps very differently. When I think about it, I continued to raise her after his death for very selfish reasons. We were already well versed in the trauma that her behavior had caused each of us while my late husband was alive. I knew it could only progress when he was no longer here to help regulate and keep some balance with her in the house. I can still hear myself saying, I just want to see her win in life. I thought love could conquer the illness, but in this instance, love would not be enough.

To show the love I thought she needed, I always used the tools learned from all the therapy we participated in and a lot of tools I learned from my current husband. Whenever my son would experience an emotional outbreak because of anger from the death of his dad, my current husband, could always calm with a hug, and he would just melt in his arms. After seeing this act, I attempted to use it in one of the worst moments my daughter had with her brother. I made the mistake of walking away from them when I felt the negative energy rising, but I told them to stay put. She said something disrespectful to me and my son, while sitting at the table doing his homework, he proceeded to correct her saying, "Be quiet and do what mommy told you." She called him stupid. I heard the commotion from upstairs and literally jumped down two flights of steps because I could feel the shift in the air. By the time I got to the kitchen, she was already throwing steak knives at his back. He was in the corner trying to protect himself. I was able to grab her to stop and then she took off to the laundry in the basement. I checked his back, hugged him, and told him I was so sorry for walking away. I took him to my husband, who was in the basement playing music, so he did not hear anything. I briefed him quickly and my son stayed with him, while I went to the laundry room to get her. I am sure she was expecting me to holler at her, while during her hysteria, however, it took all I had to pivot towards her and pull her in towards me for a hug. It was not me but the love of God that took over in that moment because my flesh just wanted to call the crisis line to have her evaluated and admitted to a facility.

I don't know why I left them downstairs. I should have listened to my gut, but I second guessed myself once again. Now, my husband was in the basement playing music and did not hear all the commotion. When she got loud, I think we all had a way of ignoring her because it was our norm. So, after she ran to the laundry room, I snatched my son to safety and took him to my husband and briefly told him what happened. I was upset with her at the moment. Listening to her complain about how I always defend him, pissed me off, because in my head I'm like, "Girl, you just threw steak knives at his back, I should be whipping your ass right now," but instead of verbalizing that, I hugged her. During that, it triggered a thought for me; how did my son feel in that instance? Did he think she wasn't going to be punished because he didn't witness my usual discipline and phone call to the crisis line for such dangerous and possible deadly behavior? She should have been seen by a crisis rep that night with a potential overnight stay at Rockford or Meadowwood for these actions. Her therapist and my husband suggested I pivot towards her in those moments. I was so messed up at times that even with a small issue, I would immediately respond as if the incident were extreme. So, I thought to myself, how was I going to pivot in a worst situation. Everything she did felt extreme to me. My natural response was going from 0 to 100 quickly. Sometimes, we look at children's behavior as attention seeking. My daughter's motive was always, let's take the attention from who has it, by her acting up and acting out.

I was getting to a place where I did not blame her for the way she was behaving. I learned to get over the disappointment of our current position and accept His appointment by positioning me in her life for a specific reason. Although there was an elixir of hate, it did not remain: It was still driven out by love.

Love is what it took for me to get to a place to let her go and rescind my guardianship. Letting her go signified failure, grief, loss of investment, broken dreams, and emotional disconnect. A principle I learned from church when dealing with marriages was, "dying to self", and the truth of the matter, I had to die to self in order to take the steps to let my daughter go.

There were clinicians that referred to her or this type of mental illness being untreatable, but because of this mental illness, I never felt she was unlovable. Watching other people around me struggle with the same sickness allowed me to have compassion after she tried to stab her brother with steak knives. The more I heard myself speak about these incidents; I became unhealthier. I was so focused on making sure Baby Girl overcame this illness, I was jeopardizing everyone else's peace, freedom, and in some scenarios, our lives. However, I realized this was a huge mistake a lot of us made. We kept unhealthy or dangerous people around us, regardless of the relationship, and before we know it, it's too late, someone is dead as a result of the sickness. It was truly the

Blood of Christ that was covering our family and kept us during these times. But the long-term effects on the family was something I would have never imagined.

She was so devoid of love. I could fill her daily with love and it was still never enough for her. This was the brokenness this sickness carried that I allowed to trickle into my life.

I knew we were no longer good for each other, but my flesh did not want to receive it.

My vision was so blurred with my expectation of wanting her to win in life, I disregarded her ability to accept the responsibility of wanting to win for herself. 1 Corinthians 13: 4-7 (NIV) 4 Love is patient and kind. Love is not jealous or boastful or proud 5 or rude. It does not demand its own way. It is not irritable, and it keeps no record of being wronged. 6 It does not rejoice about injustice but rejoices whenever the truth wins out. 7 Love never gives up, never loses faith, is always hopeful, and endures through every circumstance. This scripture was the premise behind me constantly forgiving and letting go and was my motivation to continue to stand with her and fight against this mental illness. However, no matter the condition of my love, it would not be good enough because I was not who she wanted love from. The love she always desired was from her biological mother or those who showed no interest in her.

When I think about love, I have my own definition. I moved in what was her perspective of love. Her definition of love was receiving gifts. For example, regardless of her age, she loved to play with dolls and Legos, she loved to eat out and shop. I could not believe I tried to show her love in this manner. Now, I would not do this with her siblings, especially if their behavior did not warrant it. So, I had to question myself, why was I going against my own principles? This wasn't me. I was losing my identity and going against the structure of my parenting beliefs. By this time, I was tired of advocating and fighting. One family response was, "Oh now, you're tired?" just to make light of what they knew was a heavy decision for me to even consider.

At the end of 2015, we were introduced to who we considered, one of the best therapists we have encountered. She did well with treating the entire family. She was the first therapist who introduced us to Trauma-Focused Cognitive Behavioral Therapy, which is an evidence-based treatment for children and adolescents impacted by trauma and their parents and caregivers. Research states that TF-CBT successfully resolves a broad array of emotion and behavior difficulties associated with single, multiple, and complex trauma experiences. Unfortunately, Baby Girl did not fully benefit from this service because she ran away during the process. There was one incident where my oldest daughter was back in town and I asked her to get her sister to her appointment. While waiting for her visit to end, my daughter said she left to get something to eat. About 20 minutes into the visit, I received a call from the therapist asking if Baby Girl was coming to her session today. Apparently, she walked into the door and stood there long enough for my daughter to pull off then ran away. This was about 5:20pm. Oh my gosh! I was so sick of her actions at this point! I ended up at the local Police station for hours before they put out a Gold Alert for a missing child. We finally received a call about 11pm that was found on the other side of town. Of course, the therapist and the police recommended she be seen at the local residential treatment facility.

I came to the realization I needed to get out of her way and let go. I wasn't sure what that meant at the time that I spoke into the atmosphere. Would I allow her to go and live with her God family? Would I turn her over to the state or attempt it with biological mom again? Although she already showed some extremely detrimental behaviors, she ran away often in 2016, I was still in cancer treatment and recovering from the overall experience. It came to a head for me. I remember conversing with my older daughter, and she was trying to school me on why it was necessary to let go and to know I've done all I could to help Baby Girl and I had no reason to feel guilty. I knew what I needed to do, but it warmed my heart to hear my daughter's heart towards the matter. She has always been a sweet, soft spoken individual that exuded love, compassion, joy, and friendship. People her age were drawn to her. We always had a bunch of young girls and boys at the house because of her great personality and they enjoyed being in our home. She was active at church with teaching the dance ministry and becoming an anointed praise dancer, who's gift set the atmosphere on fire. We called her our young evangelist, because she always had me picking up her friends for church. She brought more people to the church than all us adults. She always showed respect. She was active in sports, becoming one of the top volleyball players, where her skills earned her scholarships and took her across the country, playing in Costa Rica and England. In spite of all the venom we received because of Baby Girl's behavior, my oldest daughter never laid a hand on her and didn't like using the word hate. But she had a strong dislike for how she saw me being treated. And it frustrated her because I always continued to do nice things when she should not have been rewarded for bad behavior. I think my daughter was at her breaking point with watching me care for her sister, who she felt did not care for me.

At the end of 2016, I developed the courage to say, "Yes, I'm ready to let go." So, we had a family meeting to discuss the next steps to move in that direction. It was liberating when I left the courthouse from filing paperwork to rescind my guardianship. I thought I would never reach this place, after all we endured. As the days grew closer to our court date, in mid-December, I needed to remind Baby Girl that on that day she was not coming home with me. I was releasing her to her God mom, which is what she wanted. We also had talks with our son to explain that soon the household would be much different, without both of his sisters, as my oldest daughter was already in her third year of college. He was just 12 at the time and acted as if he was not bothered. Regardless of what he encountered with her, she was still his sister and he loved her too. The date arrived and I think the household was anxious except for my husband. He was in support and wanted to ensure we were good. I had her help to pack all her belongings into 4 large suitcases a couple nights before. That morning, we stopped at My mother's so she could tell could say good-bye. She cried, and it seemed very heartfelt and genuine. Arriving at court that day, reminded me of the day when my late husband was granted custody and left with her in 2003. While in the courtroom, it became pretty tense with her biological mom because she thought Baby Girl would automatically go back to her because she was her mother, but the Judge made it clear that it was not that simple. The Judge stated that, "Mrs. Faucett-Robinson spent years providing Baby Girl with proper treatment" and she wanted to ensure that treatment would continue. Her mother was in total disagreement, stating that Baby Girl didn't need any help. Now, for whatever reason, the Judge asked me the following question, "Mrs. Faucett-Robinson are you sure that you want to continue to rescind your guardianship?" I turned to my right, where her biological mom was sitting and right behind her was my daughter and her hands were in the praying position, begging me to keep her. I placed my head down and gently answered the question with a whisper and I said, "No." Her biological mom snapped and walked out of the courtroom and my daughter and I traveled back home. Everyone was surprised, but my husband. He didn't think I was ready.

The journey continued, with another incident that occurred when we were at our temporary home, since we were displaced for 17 months due to a fire that started at our neighbor's home. She was attending a new charter school, and due to her educational challenges, we were provided with special busing privileges. Well, she hated that and did everything she could not to ride, what she called, "the short bus". On this morning, she got up with an attitude and was moving slow, to the point where she missed the bus, and I was going to have to take her to school again. Unbeknownst to me, she had a packed suitcase at the bottom of the steps near the front door. Now, this was a 3-story townhome with a 1-car garage. I worked from home at the time and my desk was on the 2<sup>nd</sup> floor in the family room area. So, I could not see the front door since it was around the corner and down the steps. She got disrespectful with me as I could hear her voice fading because she was already in motion down the stairs. She referred to me taking my time to take her to school. I got up to address her and caught her at the bottom of the steps with a suitcase, and told me that, "I'm leaving." I looked at her and told her, "Do not come back!" I was just too tired to even put up a chase. That day she convinced a boy's parents she was being abused and they picked her up and took her to the school with her suitcase without attempting to call me. I found out when she arrived and the charter school, since they called me immediately. After speaking with a therapist, it was recommended I take her to the facility again, because I did not want to take her home at this point. She would go on to spend several additional visits at the treatment center due to her actions.

I made the call to DFS advising them I was preparing to let her go and to see what steps they could offer to assist me in this matter. We pulled in the entire team including myself and my husband, grandparents, her family-based therapist, her social worker, the PBH worker, And my daughter was on the phone, calling in from one of the mental health treatment facility. It became too overwhelming when she ran away and being inappropriate with strangers. The resources that were in place for our family broke down and no one was safe anymore. I didn't know what she would be capable of doing if she felt like I was restricting her freedom. She walked away from the school grounds in the middle of the day and was gone for five days with only one outfit she had on her back. I attempted to have a gold alert placed, however, the police did not do it because she had been considered a habitual runaway at this point, they would only take my information and did a missing person's report.

Again, I sat in the police department for hours. I spent some time praying, of course I was angry and then there was a moment where I wasn't very concerned, because I felt like she knew exactly what she was doing. The next day I got a call from the School Resource Officer (SRO) advising me that Baby Girl was in school and she was attending her classes. I remember asking him if he could have her go in the office and hold her there. Based on what happened, I did not want to be the one to come pick her up, so I called the police department. However, they did not get involved. The school SRO continued to call me several times letting me know my daughter had been seen on the premises but was avoiding him. Once he spoke with her, he told me he kindly asked her to go home and do the right thing. This made no sense to me. I don't understand why he just didn't contain her since she was considered a runaway. She advised the SRO, that she had been staying with a young man who didn't live too far from the school, and she shared how she was intimate with the young man and that she was going back there again to stay the night. I just cannot wrap my head around why the officer kept calling me instead of containing my daughter. Now, you may be wondering why I didn't just go to the school and pick her up at this point, I knew it would become too volatile for me, so I did not want to intervene. I knew she was too far gone. She continued to run throughout the school that day without anyone intervening based on her runaway status. I have spoken with the school psychologist, the principal and they just wanted to get her safely off the premises before school was over. She made a call to her Godbrother which I advised the school that under no circumstances should he be able to pick her up because he is not on the list. I'll later changed my mind because I didn't want to pick her up, and the police were of no assistance. I was fed up, confused and exhausted, so I told them, sure let him pick her up. I did not want her back in the house at all, but her god brother called because she wanted to come pick up a few things. I packed her bags and allowed them to come into my home where he got disrespectful with me because he was believing everything my daughter was telling him and some stuff she was making up. I checked him, then I told him they had to get out of my house. This was just too much.

She had the nerve to call me back and asked me, could she go to my mother's house and pick up her stuff from there. Her Godbrother didn't like my response and he interjected and said something else; by the time I snapped in the most calm and respectful way, advising him that he's needs to know his place because I raised her for 15 years. He needed to show respect because, regardless of his age, he was still a child to me. I hung up, told my husband, which he later addressed him man-to-man.

Our daughter lacked empathy to show genuine love for anyone and I was too drained to keep extending my love, that had no value to her. So, we formally proceeded with the process of rescinding my guardianship, which started with a huge family session at my mother's home, with her new therapist guiding the process. This was very interesting because the godbrother's girlfriend had so much to say, she kept saying, "Oh, she ain't gonna do none of that with us.", also said, "Y'all got to many restrictions , she need to have some freedom." Now, some of the family interjected, and I chuckled and simply reminded her that "We've been in this for 15 years and you might want to listen to some wisdom." But she was relentless. We didn't have anything to prove. If it's one thing I know is that the mental illness would show up after the honeymoon period ended. That night was the official family goodbye, as we allowed her to leave and walk out of my mother's home with her god family. Although I was hurt, there was a sense of relief. We appeared in court once again in December of 2016, along with her biological mom and god mom, and the Judge asked me where I felt was the best place for my daughter. I opted for her god family since they did love Baby Girl, but I didn't think it was the best option because I felt the time we invested into her success would fall backwards, because they allowed her to do what she wanted. Apparently, they believed her lies that we were mistreating her. By the end of the year, the Godbrother saw me in the mall, humbled himself and apologized to me as he admitted Baby Girl had them convinced that she was being mistreated. But they found out first-hand after she had gone to live with them, that Baby Girl was not telling the truth about us.

I learned the following and would like my readers to know that:

1. You never have to defend yourself, especially when you are doing the right thing.
2. Regardless of the rejection you may experience, remember you are always enough.
3. Be your own advocate until you find what works for you and your family.

# CHAPTER 9
# FINDING SHEA

Nothing reveals who you are more than your response to the pressures you experience in life. I learned my tolerance level was very high, and my capacity to endure multiple levels of pain was greater than I knew. Therefore, I learned to be what my Pastor called me, "wounded healer," meaning no matter what loss occurred in my life, what abuse was endured, what obstacles challenged me, or what trauma tried to overtake me, I did not allow it to stop me from moving in purpose. I often heard the phrase, "Shea, you're so strong," however, I displayed many moments of weakness, and there were moments when I lost sight of me and the things I needed to thrive. So, I share with you a few things that worked to bring me up from those lowly places and some things I learned in the process.

## Stronger than I Knew

Let me reflect a little on my first marriage. Although, I grew up around Sickle Cell disease with my aunt who lived with severe symptoms of this debilitating illness, I could not assume our family's experience with my aunt would be the same for me and my late husband. When we were engaged, I remember my maternal grandmother saying to me, "Girl, you better not marry that boy with that disease and you better not have any children with him!" I chuckled, when my aunt spoke up and said, "Mom, you can't tell her what to do!" But I didn't take it personal, because my grand mom was simply speaking her truth based on her experience of caring for her daughter. I respected what she was trying to express, as she did not want me taking on this disease, she knew first-hand was brutal to watch your loved one endure. I trusted God in the matter and prayed that our experience with this disease would not be my grandmother's experience. I may have been naïve, but I have to say that I was all in with my marriage, regardless of what was to come with marrying a man with such a harsh illness. I gave 100% to loving, encouraging, supporting and caregiving for my late husband, so much I forgot about my own self-care and pursing the things I wanted.

So, I started with my marriage, because this played a major role in me losing myself especially as the Sickle Cell Disease progressed in my late husband's life. For example, I dreamed of going back to finish my college degree, but I did not see a way for me to pursue it due to pure exhaustion of our daily routine. Although, my late husband was very supportive and kept pushing me to register for school, he did not realize what most of my nights consisted of, especially whenever his pain medicine would overtake him and alter his thought process. What my late husband did not know is that along with the normal tasks of being a wife, and mother, that my days after work, I was left with monitoring him, because he would often hurt himself or unintentionally destroy some of the electronics or other property in the house. The combination of medicine would take him on a high, where he would try to fix things in the house that were not broken and in that process the item would get broken. It was a fight trying to stop my late husband when he was in that zone, because he was so strong, so I would switch up and speak softly to him to try and guide him to sit in a chair if possible, at least until his body relaxed. There were times that medicine would knock him right in his tracks, therefore, I would wake up and find him passed out anywhere in the home which was very frightening. It was an overwhelming task attempting to hide these moments from my children. There were many moments where I thought I would wake up and realize my worst nightmare had come true. My late husband spent about 14 days of the month in the hospital when the sickness heightened in his body. So, you can probably imagine the weight it placed on the family, especially me. I was the one running back and forth to the hospital with the children, taking him his needs or breakfast, lunch, and dinner, since hated the hospital food. I was meeting everyone else's needs but my own.

To get back to me and the things I needed, I had to pray for my heart, which became bitter. I was reminded of how I represented myself in love. Walking in bitterness and hatred was not my character. I made the commitment, that I would love for better or for worse, I accepted my position to continue to serve in that capacity and forgave myself for what I deemed as falling out of love with him. After continual prayer, my heart and the full love towards my late husband was restored.

In the midst of feeling failed by the health system to help my daughter, I found myself experiencing my own health challenge. April 29 while doing my own breast examination in the shower, I found the tiny lump above my left breast. It was hard as a rock. And based on what I learned in the past, I merely thought to myself, could this be cancer? So, I immediately went into to prayer, later fasting, and laying prostrate before the Lord and declaring that it wasn't cancer. I went to have my first biopsy around May 6th. The two-week waiting period was the longest ever. I thought to myself, why does it take two weeks to get this result? Why would they do that to me or anybody? But again, declared that it wasn't cancer, and it didn't matter. I knew this was just a test of my faith and I believed beyond a shadow of a doubt, that it was not cancer. Then, I was called back before the first results to get a Fine Needle Aspiration.

Talk about fear coming over me. It was official on May 19, 2015; I was diagnosed with breast cancer, 4 days before my birthday. Wow! Happy Birthday to Me! Nevertheless, I did not allow this news to depress me. I decided on that day I would survive this, and I was about to go on this journey to help someone else. Believing I would survive, I shared this with my children in a joyous and confident manner. I was determined not to show any fear and trust the Word of God, otherwise, they would not believe. My son's initial response was, "I can't lose my mother too." Well, I was going to put up a fight, because they were not going to lose me too. I changed my eating habits and made healthier decisions for my body, with consistent exercise, making healthy shakes, added more protein to my diet according to my situation. One huge change was getting plenty of rest. I endured two major and two minor surgeries, and I was set for Chemotherapy after my surgeries and then Radiation shortly afterwards. After my second cocktail of chemo, I remained very weak for several days. On September 3, 2015, I had with a fever of 104 degrees and could barely walk. I was rushed to see my doctor and it was determined that my port was infected. My doctor immediately removed the port from my chest in her office and discovered that it was full of puss. My surgeon sent me to the ER with the understanding that I would receive antibiotics for 24 hours only. However, I remained in the hospital for 7 days. I got weaker and I could not eat anything until day 6, hence, losing 12 pounds in the process. I never lost hope, even though the staff could not identify the type infection to give me proper treatment, I still had a drive to survive. I was going to win the fight.

One September 10, 2015, the same date I was discharged from the hospital, my current husband and younger daughter were in our home when a fire from our neighbors' home interrupted their sleep around 3am in the morning. I left the hospital and returned to no home. I was very grateful to be alive and for the life of my husband and daughter. At this point, I believe we all were thinking, how much more can we endure? That evening, we stayed at a hotel for about 2 weeks then moved to a temporary home, where we were displaced for 17 months. We moved back into our home on January 31, 2017. Through it all, we remained prayerful, humble, hopeful, and grateful. We did not allow the negative circumstances to destroy or separate us, but it brought us closer and made us stronger in that moment. You would never know what we were going through. We used joy as our strength to endure the rough times.

When I think back on how prayer helped me overcome the trying moments in my first marriage when Sickle Cell dominated my life, I could only think and believe that if God did it for me then, He would do it for me now in this fight against cancer.

## Forgive, Let Go, and Heal

My challenges with raising Baby Girl showed me I was not as good as people thought I was, as I made some bad choices and decisions. I always asked myself when faced with any trial, was I going to quit or press into the next level. I asked myself in this scenario with raising Baby Girl, what story would I tell the people? Would I be "Completely Transparent"? Will I allow people to see my flaws? I submitted and said, "Yes," because again, my story is not my own. Our experiences are designed to encourage, inspire, and motivate others out of their challenges, or maybe learn some do's and don'ts.

It was funny because during the mess we were enduring, my mother still did not know how bad things were for me personally. She told me I always had this strong façade, and the way I tried to manage and control everything, it comes off as me being okay. I guess, it goes back to that phrase of, "Shea, you're so strong." I cringed when I heard it because I would say to myself, "Don't they know? Can they see my pain?" I gave Baby Girl's behavior so much space in my life, I didn't have any space for me or anyone else for that matter. I wanted so badly to help her heal through this process that I selfishly neglected what I needed and what was best for my family. This ended up being detrimental to everyone who played a role in her life. As, I am writing, Beyoncé's song, "beautiful nightmare," popped in my head, because at times my life had become just that, a beautiful nightmare. Overall, I mean, I thought my life was lovely, but I tell you it was mind-blowing, some of the abusive, backstabbing, brutal, hateful, and disgusting challenges that were presented. I knew it was overwhelming and I was losing myself in moments, when my natural sweet, loving, compassionate and never give up attitude felt unnatural. I despised the fact that I wanted to return to her, the same pain that she gave out. But I learned from husband, who worked in the field human services, I needed to learn to separate her from the behavior she was displaying. Now, I thought I knew that, but on that day, it resonated in deeply in my soul and that was the beginning of me letting go and not holding on to the anger and resentment I had towards my daughter.

Breakthrough in my mind occurred, therefore, I was able to view each crisis afterwards, with more compassion. Although it was still frustrating, I did my best to not be as high-strong about the situation, which created a less stressful experience. I found my pure self and share the essence of love that was instilled in me. Love is what I felt like and what I have always represented. It was my being. To me, finding me was all about displaying who I was, which was love. I just have this natural love for people, which is why I enjoy serving in ministry, the love of helping and giving. A part of finding me was identifying those things I didn't bury, which was my giving spirit, this helped to sustain me throughout this time. So, I gave, and I gave, and I gave, whether it was hundreds of hours to volunteering to multiple organizations, supporting my family and friend whenever in need, just showing up, it's what I did to show my love. Although I was always in the mode of meeting someone else' needs, I discovered that when I was struggling, I think I became more intentional about my giving. I often heard, "you need to slow down", "you're doing too much and "you need to rest." And I got it, as far as not getting the proper rest. But the level of giving was part of who I was. It is still who I am.

A few things I learned in finding myself:

1. Do not give negativity space in your life.
2. Never allow any tough circumstances to stop you from living a productive and fruitful life.
3. Make time to love you: your love is enough.
4. Remain true to who are and what makes you happy.

# CHAPTER 10
# EMOTIONAL JEOPARDY:

I have done a lot of sharing from my perspective, and in searching out myself, I have come to realize It wasn't just about me and my experience. So, in this chapter you will read from the Vantage Point of other family members who had direct or indirect encounters with Baby Girl.

**Her Dad:** I found a note pad from my late husband where he wrote, "I will not allow my daughter to continue disrespecting my wife in this manner." On that page, he had bullets points with locations of mental health facilities on other information. Jimmy was no nonsense like his Pop. He felt a like a beating was the cure all for Baby Girl's behavior. At times, when I would ask him not to beat her, he reminded by saying, "My mother beat the hell out of me, and I had Sickle Cell, she ain't going to die. And that was it. I know how he expressed the stress of raising Baby Girl caused him to have more frequent Sickle Cell Crises. So, I guess that would have been his emotional jeopardy: The impact on his health.

**Cousin:** She reminds me of myself sometimes, that's why she listens to me

**Sister:**

After the death of my Mr. Jimmy, I felt like I needed to protect my mom and brother from my sister. If I stayed around, I could keep my mom from possibly blacking out again or responding in a negative way that could potentially risk her freedom. I was afraid my sister would try to harm my mom or brother in their sleep, especially now that Mr. Jimmy was gone. I even considered going to college locally because I felt obligated and responsible for the protection of my family. My mother told me, "No" and reminded me about vision and dream to go out of state for school. She said she did not want any of her children to hold the weight of her decision to keep raising my sister. Also, it did bother me when I talked to my friends about my experience, they always thought I was being mean, and I was the problem. This made me angry because they looked at me like I was wrong, until they saw how she behaved. I was just concerned because I did not want my mom or sister to harm one another, because Baby Girl was disrespectful with her mouth to be a little person.

**Big brother**

I didn't necessarily have encounters with her, well at least no negative encounters. It was sort of like she always put on innocence when I was around. I'm not sure if she did that to probably have that person that only saw her in a good light. I think the Jeopardy of that was, what did I do or what didn't do to help the situation? It made me think like, "ma'am! what if I had been around one or two more times, maybe I could've help with those interventions put in place for her." Or the fear of what would happen if she went crazy and I was around. How would I handle that? Trying not to come to her aid was difficult because she did present herself as this perfect child in front of me. When certain things were said about her, it was hard to accept because I have never seen that person. So of course, I had an understanding that the person who does ninety-nine wrong things will make sure to glorify the one good thing.

Whenever she would ask me about participating or me taking her somewhere fun, I would always follow up with my parents first and 99% of the time the response was always, "No, she can't go and she can't participate." In my head I was like, "Well, she is still a kid!"

The Jeopardy that she cost me was confliction in myself and as a young man. I had to ask myself, Is she a wolf in sheep's clothing? But one thing she never did with me was hide the truth. If I asked her about what she's was accused of, she would admit to doing it. So, if the gloves fit, what am I supposed to do? I tried not to aid her in her process of thinking. Now that she has been removed from the situation, the family is still experiencing the impact in addition to new impacts that have been identified.

Hopefully, what's been shared in this book can shed some light allow people to express themselves appropriately and let go.

**Younger Brother**

I don't remember all the stuff my sister did to me when I was younger. But I do remember trying to get away with acting like her when I was mad. I hit my Mom in the face once. Well, that didn't turn out well. And I realized it was wrong. I did not like it when I my sister got aggressive with my mom and sometimes, I did get angry and wanted to hurt her, but my mom told me not to put my hands on her. So, I just had to watch and tell my her to stop acting up.

**Pop-pop (deceased):** Pop was a no nonsense when It came to discipline. He always stuck to his guns. For him, I don't believe there was any emotional jeopardy. His modo was, "Put these hands to her @@&". That's it, plain and simple for him.

**Mom-mom (deceased)** – She was his pride and joy, and when Baby Girl came into the picture, she was overjoyed, because her first born son now has a biological daughter. Even though she witnessed many of the Baby Girl's behaviors, she did whatever she could do to protect her from getting in trouble.

**Uncle:** I told my sister-in-law that she doesn't owe my brother anything by keeping her. If anything, she should have let her go a long time ago.

**My Husband:** Although we had a wonderful wedding and was able to get a way for our honeymoon, I felt that mental illness destroyed the honeymoon period in our marriage, because of many trips to the crisis center, school visits, therapy sessions and outbreaks that stole our time. I felt a degree of resentment towards my wife. I felt we were held emotionally and mentally hostage by our daughter's actions. We were unable to socialize her because of her hyper sexuality and poor boundaries. It hindered the desire to want to be intimate with one another because of the pure exhaustion of the everyday dealing with the behavior and mental illness. Her negative energy NEVER dissipated. It felt like the foundation of our marriage had been tribulation. We left for a honeymoon and came back to hell.

While I was aware of the extent of her dysfunction, her whole body was trauma induced to the point that she would seek comforts in physical pleasure, because she lacked self-soothing traits, or healthy intimacy. I do feel that as people of color, we cannot take trauma off. We wear trauma in our bodies, which is part of the reason we endure. For our daughter, life introduced her to reality.

**Her cousin:** I thought her behavior was shocking but thought she must have a reason for acting the way she did. So, yes, I pre-judged y'all first.

**My deceased brother and sister-in-law** played a big part when they lived around the corner from us, which was also a huge help because they gave my mom and I a break from all the pressure. Baby Girl always showed these angel-like behaviors for them. It was strange, so I would say they did not experience any emotional jeopardy.

**Family member (great aunt):** I found her to be very loving, compassionate, concerned. She negated love with material things. It was always, what can I get from you? I never saw her make a connection or sustain connections. I know a child can understand empathy at the age of 6, but she had no empathy for the people around her. She didn't know how to love anyone else but herself. Whenever I had her with me, she required 24/7 attention. She was 15 years-old at the time and you had to stay in her presence.

**Mom-mom (Mom M.):**

I was always on heightened alert when Baby Girl was with me. I had to make sure that she did not place herself in a position where something could happen to her. I saw it taking a toll on everyone in your household and with your parents. The behaviors were so demonic at times it wore me down to the bones. There were times when there was a feeling of doom when she was around. The best way I could explain, was it felt like a constant heaviness. Although I could have fun with her, you could not relax in that environment. I was concerned for the safety of everyone in your home, so, I always prayed for y'all. We stayed on alert because we never knew when she was going to drop a bomb. My jeopardy came from feeling bad as a Christian and as a person that I had negative feelings towards her being a child.

**Baby Girl-** Her emotional jeopardy stemmed from the absence of being unable to bond with her biological Mom as an infant. The lack of this action may cause an infant to develop psychopathologies.

I personally interviewed Baby Girl on 7-11-20. She later realized she needed people like us around her to support. She said the behavior she displayed only pushed people away from her. She made the comparison regarding her thought process then and now. When she lived with us, she thought I was just in her business, but now she sees I was trying to get her the support needed for her success. She mentioned how she misses the way we would check on her and was concerned about what was going on in her life. She missed the structure we provided, even though she always fought against us. She missed how we made sure she was doing her homework, made sure her meds were straight and did what was necessary to ensure her educational needs were in order. She took the love and structure we provided as a means of us not liking her, but she now realizes is what she needed. She understood she was acting out and running away from her problem. **When I asked if she thought I really love her she replied**: "To an extent". I asked what she meant by that and she replied she recognized the love I had for her, but she pushed it away with all she did to me.

**During a separate interview, I wanted to get her perspective and asked what life is like for her living with this thing called mental illness and if you really felt loved by me?**

She replied, "yeah and no! I thought there was always favoritism between me and my brother because he was your child, and you cared more about him than you did me. It wasn't fair because I had disabilities that no one really understood. I didn't know what was wrong with me and I didn't understand why I was acting this way."


**Mom-mom:** I didn't trust her because she was a liar and a manipulator. Because she was a very sexual person, I never felt comfortable leaving her around my husband alone, in fear of what she may say or accuse him of doing something. So, this caused me to take some extreme measures based on behaviors that I witnessed. There were some unimaginable things which is why I put measures in place to never leave her alone with anything or anyone while in my home. Although I loved her and some of the things about her, I often struggled with liking her beautiful personality, but then there were parts about her that were very ugly, that I didn't like. It was a Jekyll and Hyde type of thing. You never knew what you were going to get at any given time. Because I witnessed various personalities, I felt like it was hard to know how I could feel about her. Having her around created a lot of responsibility. we had to watch everything she did, we had to be careful as to what we said around her because she would use that information against us at times. I did my best to treat her fairly like my other grandchildren. For example, buying the same number of gifts as the others so no one would feel slighted even when she didn't deserve it, I still wanted her to feel loved and like she belonged. But these were things I would not do if you didn't deserve it. But I made these exceptions to make her feel good, which was not a good decision. Part of my jeopardy caused me to go against my own basic principles regarding rewarding children for bad behavior. Her behavior created a division amongst family because some could not understand why we were so strict at times with her. So, we had to deal with being judged by our own family members because of our reaction to her, which did not feel good at all. Because of the love we had for her, we easily got caught up in her lies which caused us to second-guess each other.

**Me** – I reached my breaking point. As caterers, we owned several sets of specialized knives. They were very sharp. The slightest touch would slice your finger. I woke up early one morning to prepare breakfast. It must have been a Saturday because I wasn't preparing for work, nor was I preparing for church. I pulled out our special knives so I could cut up some fruit to make a fruit salad. Suddenly, I felt this weight on my body. I remember gasping for air because it felt like I was kicked in the stomach. Trauma attacked my brain, playing tricks on me, telling me I was not good enough. I could not explain why I was feeling this way. I had never been in this place before. Then I remember hearing, I guess in my head that "my life didn't matter." I was just so weak and sick and tired of my life not being where I wanted it to be. I just remember whimpering, "I'm too young to have all this stress on me." The tears started flowing uncontrollably. I could hear my voice telling me to pick up the knife and cut my throat, but there was the stable part of me that was thinking, "If I cut my throat, I will die." I was terrified because the voice became more pronounced. To shut the voice down, I cried and shouted, "Jesus!" I cried out to the Father and thanked God because the Holy Spirit moved me to call my mom. I mustered up enough strength in that moment to make the call.

I don't remember what my mom said to me, but I felt better knowing I exposed the shame of what I was about to attempt. I hung up the phone a lot stronger, knowing I needed to pray and worship. I realized I could not allow the enemy to silence my voice, because he would snatch the victory from me and that would impact our legacy and generations to come. I was immediately reminded that my family needed me whole. The words from my Pastor's sermon, was that someone will need to be the sacrificial lamb or sacrifice for the family, and I reluctantly accepted I was the sacrifice for our family. I had no choice but to endure this process. So, I returned to what I knew best and that was to use some of the following tools:

- My grandmother, who lived to be 100 years-old, taught me the power of prayer and how to praise, which is my greatest weapon.

- My mother taught me how to press through, nothing could stop her.
- My brothers taught me to fight to win.
- My Life experience was teaching me how to push to overcome.
- Only the word of God was going to teach me to heal.

With God's Saving Grace on my life and after applying these tools, my mind shifted almost immediately, as needed to get out of that depressive state. It was like driving a 5-speed vehicle, the shift was necessary to get to the next level and accelerate quickly away from that place. See, I knew some the of risk I was taking by marrying my first husband with a debilitating illness, but I was all in, as I opted to make that choice. However, I DID NOT raise my hand to deal with mental illness and abuse from a child. This just compiled more tension on me as the caregiver for both. This was my emotional Jeopardy, as I almost took my life, when God said my story was designed to help save. I was reminded of the song, "I Give Myself Away." One verse says. "My life is not my own, to you I belong, I give myself away, so you can use me." How could I be used if I decided to destroy life?

**What I have learned:**

Whenever you are dealing with any form of mental illness, please ensure to engage the proper team for guidance and support. It is crucial to get assistance for the entire family and not just the diagnosed individual. You cannot help to guide the one person towards a healing journey without helping to heal the whole tribe, otherwise, it would just cause a reinfection in the camp and destroy the roots where growth was taking place. This is a critical step because the effects from the induced trauma can cause others to duplicate some behaviors which occurred in our younger son, and just the harmful influences that it could have over one's mind.

**What I want my readers to know:** I have listed some useful resources if anyone is experience challenges with trauma as it relates to mental illness, abuse, depression, and suicide:

- www.Nimh.nih.gov
- www.Suicidepreventionlifeline.org

Shea C. Robinson

# CHAPTER 11
# UNRESOLVED SOLUTIONS:

## Held on for what?

Why did you stick out for so long, someone asked? I felt like I was her last option. Her mom walked away and no one on her mother's or father's side wanted anything to do with her at the time. Her dad was now gone, and the impacts of her behavior burned so many bridges that even those who cared for her, were very apprehensive with trying to maintain a close relationship. Fighting for her to win over mental illness, was like me standing in the gap for many little girls who did not have anyone stand up for them. That was it! So, this was one reason I advocated so hard. I felt like she wasn't going to make it if we let her go. All the investment was made to get her the proper help to reach success, would be reversed if she were not under our guidance. We wanted her to at least graduate from high school and protect her from teenage pregnancy because I knew as soon as she got the freedom she desired, it was over, she was going to try to get pregnant based on what she always shared with us.

Because family and friends could not grasp why I was holding on, one of the main statements or questions that was asked was, "Do you feel obligated to keep her because of the loyalty and love you have for my first husband, Jimmy?" My response was, "Absolutely Not!" I have written documentation from my late husband stating that and I quote, "I will not continue to allow my daughter to disrespect my wife," along with facilities he was looking into for residential treatment for our daughter. So, based on that, I never felt guilty or obligated to keep her. My late husband knew how challenging it was and how her rage was mainly directed towards me. Again, it was all set around wanting to set her up to win in life. I got my family on board with confessing she would win. It was my competitive nature, although there's no competition, I think I allowed my winning mentality to take over and become dominant in my decision making. And for me, I depended on my faith, prayer, and continued family support for Baby Girl to win in this journey.

As I reflected on this process, I can see how my competitive nature took over. I wanted to see her win more than she wanted it for herself. This was done at the expense of my family's peace, at the expense of my peace. The phrase, "it won't work" wasn't acceptable in my mind because with my faith, I knew anything could happen. I wanted to prove something to one of her previous doctors. All I could think was, how dare she tell me that I would never be enough for Baby Girl and to let her go immediately?" This was crazy because I wanted to prove this to a doctor, who I would never see again, that my daughter would be successful, and our love would be enough to see Baby Girl through this sickness. I bet if she could see our entire story line, she would probably tell me, "I told you so." I know, I could have saved a lot of heart ache and pain if I would have listened. But as mom and just being a good human being, I could not turn back on a child.

Wow! It really hit when I realized I was torturing the entire family, by holding on and trying to save my child who did not want to stay connected with us. I admit I made the mistake of making Baby Girl the primary focus at times, which was very unhealthy for the family. Rescinding my guardianship and letting her go was one of the healthiest solutions I could have chosen for myself and our family. But I also believe at some point I got in the way of Gods plans. I kept holding on. For what? And what I know now is, God was showing me or giving me a way out. I would not let go, but it was becoming clearer I could no longer continue to shield and protect her because she was going to keep fighting me. She belonged to God first, and it was time for me to allow Him to fully work in her life.

## Letting Go and Embracing the journey:

It took me some time allow myself to finally let go and not be worried about her outcome. I had to trust and believe the Word of God instilled in her would return to her right mind. Proverbs 22:6 states, "Train up a child in the way he should go, and when he is old, he will not depart from it." I trusted God's word and believed someday she would understand that love we were dishing out to her. For so long, I ignored the advice and suggestions of letting my daughter go because I wanted to help her walk into victory over this illness more than she wanted it for herself. So much, I jeopardized everyone's safety. I got past the fear and finally changed our story and give her the freedom she desired and allowed her to fight for her own health and well-being.

In my process of trying to finalize the book, one of my family members was asking a bunch of questions, like, "Why did you allow this, and how did that happen?" I stopped them during the questioning and said, "she's exhausting, this is exhausting and making my head hurt from the pressure of trying to gather my thoughts for an explanation. It started to touch those areas of trauma that I choose not to relive. I have learned to identify how trauma is still showing up in my life. For me in this instance, it was fear, anger, and avoidance. That avoidance is why I turned from this book project. I delayed my progress for almost two weeks because of the fear of my consciousness erupting the pain body. I got nervous, I didn't want to do the book, but I could hear my coach's voice saying, "If God gave you the book in this season, than it was designed for you to complete in this season."

I knew this book had a purpose because of the pain that was being pulled out of me. So, I mediated on all the efforts put forward to get it done. Here I was, more than 75% from completing my manuscript and I wanted to quit. I felt like I was frozen because every time I would sit down to get back into the grind, distractions came or let me say I allowed distractions to stop me because I didn't want to go forward. I was frustrated with how emotional I would become with some thoughts of going through this process, hence, this is unresolved trauma. A lot of my thoughts weren't even about the bad times, however, I still found myself feeling sad.

## Reconnecting (The beginning stage of healing)

After some months passed from the "rescind of guardianship" process, Baby Girl attempted reaching out to me. This is when I identified she had issues of trauma. Whenever, her name appeared on my phone, I would cringe, and look to my husband

and ask him, in a childlike voice, "what should I do, should I answer? I don't want to talk to her." I knew she would have a story to pull on my heartstring that would draw me back into her circle of mess. Well, I finally accepted one of her calls without any resistance, and that is when I realized I had let go of the bitterness. Forgiveness happened. Although, I felt I had already done this, I still felt resentment towards her when I would see her name pop up on my phone. But in this instance, it became easy. That unconditional love was flowing. I stopped avoiding her. I realized she still needed my guidance with some things, and I was willing to provide that, if all I had to do was talk for a little. I remember her apologizing to me for her actions. I didn't think I needed that. She did not really owe me that, but I have to say it felt good to hear, because it felt sincere. We were able to genuinely converse and laugh. It was healthy dialogue, and I was open and willing to allow this new relationship to develop.

At first, she did not know what to call me, she asked, "Do I still call you Mom or Mrs. Shea?" She asked on the day the removal of guardianship was finalized. I was so angry and hurt, I told her at that time, I said, "Don't call me anything; as a matter of fact, call me Mrs. Shea." She remembered that moment and was very unsure on what to call me today. So, when she called me Mrs. Shea, I asked, "why are you calling me that? I'm still the mother who raised you for 15 years." During that call, she apologized to me because of her actions. But I was the one who owed her an apology for behaving in that manner, because I knew that wasn't right. I was acting out of my emotions. I said, "Of course, you can call me Mom. I will always be that to you and you will always be my daughter."

However, I feel restricted in my current relationship with her today. For example, I think I still hold some resentment towards her because I won't even share some of her successes publicly like I do with my other children. She recently graduated from high school, which I was very excited for her being able to accomplish this goal. Although this a goal that we always instilled in the household, I was not comfortable enough to share. I identified this as another form of trauma. Because I have allowed her back into my life, I have been able to celebrate her in areas where I was initially repulsed to be around her.

But I found it very difficult to celebrate her publicly, because her name alone carried much grief and pain for me.

I found in this process of researching trauma, I started to experience pain in my stomach and felt very ill. During a conversation with a clinician, I was informed how women carry pain in their stomachs, which is a clear sign of the trauma being revealed or being exposed through pain in my body, so, I still have some healing to do. I realized that while I may have done a good job of pressing through the trauma and living life, I have done a very poor job of ensuring I receive the healing necessary to better myself in order to help others who have endured multiple levels of trauma.

This is a temporary solution that enables me to be able deal with or confront some of my challenges, but still unresolved because I have not healed. I believe part of my healing process, would have to incorporate her into certain areas of my life. However, I will remain guarded due to the lack of trust because of the constant manipulation that we lived under.

Even as I speak with my daughter today, I keep my social distance from her. Because of all the trauma I have endured over time, I seemed to have blocked most of the good ole days from my memory. I never stopped loving my daughter, I just distanced myself from the love I have for her to protect my peace. I learned how to live and walk through the pain, while never really processing the long-term damage until now. Actually, I did not know that any of us were severely impacted until certain actions and behaviors began to surface in our lives recently.

Although, it has been two years since I rescinded my guardianship and released from the full responsibility of caring for Baby Girl, I find it necessary to address the trauma I endured to obtain total restoration for myself. I think in doing this it will allow me to remain open to build a healthier relationship with my daughter. More importantly, I might be able to assist others in their process of healing.

I encourage my readers or anyone with similar experiences to do following:

1. Relinquish the guilt or shame of making a hard decision to maintain your peace.
2. You define the narrative of your outcome. Take back your power.
3. Seek help! It is never too late.
4. Share your story.

# AUTHOR'S BIO:

Shea graduated Summa Cum Laude with her degree in Business/Concentration in Health Services. She is an ordained minister and an avid member of Heavens Gates Ministries, the Co-Founder of the James L. Faucett III Sickle Cell 5K Walk/Run, she served as the liaison of the Sickle Cell Anemia Pillar she established to heighten the awareness of this disease within the corporation. Shea is a survivor of state 2B breast cancer, an advocate for Breast Cancer Survivors and teaches the preventions for Triple Negative Breast Cancer. Shea is a co-author in Married to the Ring Volume 1, exposing a glimpse of her spar of love and hate with caregiving for her late spouse. She has spoken on an international stage in a strategic boxing ring match sharing her battle against mental illness. She serves her community with countless volunteer hours to aid with teenage girls and the homeless. This genuine passion earned her the honorable Presidents' Volunteer Service Award for the past several years assigned by former President Barack Obama and our current President. She is also the recipient of the Governors' Outstanding Volunteer Award in Delaware. Shea loves spending time working in ministry and spending time with her family, which includes planning most of the birthday, Holiday, and special events. She finds so much joy in creating memories with family and friends by capturing all those moments on video or with beautiful still shots. The one location that released the freedom for Shea to complete this book was sitting anywhere near a body of water, which is known as her peaceful place. Shea and her husband Eric are the proud parents of 5 children and 4 grandchildren and 2 on the way.

Facebook - Shea Faucett-Robinson
Instagram – shea_720
Instagram - Posture_of_a_Pearl
Website - www.postureofapearl.com

Made in the USA
Middletown, DE
21 February 2022

61642959R00060